MORE PRAISE FOR
POWERFUL EXHIBIT MARKETING

"Barry Siskind brings fresh perspective to the face-to-face marketing experience. He guides the reader through the process from start to finish and begins by looking at objectives. Barry understands that objectives form the basis of the entire process. This is a solid read for newcomers and seasoned pros looking for new insight."

—*Michael Bandy, President, Trade Show Exhibitors Association*

"Managing the exhibit program is becoming more demanding. Barry's step-by-step approach is a must read for every serious exhibitor."

—*Lili Eigl, Communications Manager, Union des Foires Internationales (UFI)*

"*Powerful Exhibit Marketing* is an excellent primer on strategies and concepts for successful trade shows and events. Siskind offers a practical class for beginners and, at the same time, an MBA for trade show and event industry experts."

—*Anselmo Carvalho, Director, Feira&Cia Group, Publisher of the main Brazilian trade show magazine Feria&Cia (Trade Show & Co.), and Producer of Exposystems (Brazilian trade show and conference for trade shows)*

OTHER BOOKS BY BARRY SISKIND

Books for business

The Successful Exhibitor

The Successful Exhibitor's Handbook: Trade Show Techniques for Beginners & Pros

Making Contact: Master the Art of Networking to Develop New Business Needs, Uncover Hidden Opportunities & Enhance Your Career

The Power of Exhibit Marketing

Books for everyone

Bumblebees Can't Fly: 7 Simple Strategies for Making the Impossible Possible

Eagles Must Soar: 7 Simple Strategies for Living a Life with Certainty

POWERFUL
EXHIBIT
MARKETING

BARRY SISKIND

POWERFUL
EXHIBIT
MARKETING

THE COMPLETE GUIDE TO SUCCESSFUL TRADE SHOWS, CONFERENCES AND CONSUMER SHOWS

WILEY

John Wiley & Sons Canada, Ltd.

Library and Archives Canada Cataloguing in Publication

Siskind, Barry, 1946-
    Powerful exhibit marketing : the complete guide to successful trade shows, conferences and consumer shows / Barry Siskind.

Includes index.
ISBN-13 978-0-470-83469-2
ISBN-10 0-470-83469-2

1. Trade shows.	2. Marketing.	I. Title.
T396.S568 2005	659.1'52	C2005-900325-1

Production Credits:
Cover design: Natalia Burobina
Interior text design: Adrian So R.G.D.

Printer: Tri-Graphic Printing Ltd.

John Wiley & Sons Canada Ltd.
6045 Freemont Blvd.,
Mississauga, Ontario
L5R 4J3

Printed in Canada
10 9 8 7 6 5 4 3 2 1

For
Barbara

Contents

Acknowledgments

I wonder where the image of a writer sitting in a deserted room banging away on his keyboard completely oblivious to the outside world comes from? It certainly is not my experience. To write a book like this requires the thoughts, ideas, suggestions and criticism from a multitude of people. Without my outside world I simply could not do what I do.

So, here is my partial list of people to thank. If I have left your name off the list please chalk it up to a senior moment. It was not my intention.

Robert Babcock, Michael Bandy, Karen Bassel, Nancy Carroll, Anselmo Carvalho, Rob Cohen, Bernie Colterman, Bob Dallmeyer, Douglas Ducate, Ron Gooch, Robert Harris, Jeffrey Hill, Nelson Hudes, Erin Kelly, David Lee, Anthony Lindan, Robert Mackwood, Ken Mark, John McCormick, Elizabeth McCurdy, Karen Milner, Joan McKnight, Terry Palmer, John Passalacqua, Darren Rabie, John Sanginesi, Jennifer Smith, Tina Vedovat, Paul Wigfield,

As always, Jillian, Geoffrey, Mark, Robert, Cory, Suzanne, Carol, Lynda, Aidyn, Zoë, Daniel, Shaindy, Seth, Shawn, Ilmee, Esther, Cheryl and Carl. And the hundreds of show managers and thousands of exhibiting companies who have made me part of their exhibit program.

Introduction

"Before everything else,
getting ready is the secret of success."
— Henry Ford —

WHAT IS EXHIBIT MANAGEMENT?

Congratulations! You have taken the first step to becoming an exhibit manager. Now you are probably asking, "What the heck is an exhibit manager?" Good question. Exhibiting is setting up a display at a trade show, conference, sporting event, mall, hotel lobby, or in a boardroom. The exhibit manager is the person responsible for planning, organizing, and executing the exhibit plan, which begs the question, "What exhibit plan?"

Exhibiting is face-to-face marketing at such places as trade shows, consumer shows, special events, road shows, private shows, hospitality events, product launches, seminars and professional conferences. There are two essential ingredients: the hardware, and the software. Hardware refers to the actual exhibit and materials—the physical means of creating the right image and attracting the right audience. The software includes the planning and implementation of programs required to facilitate face-to-face interaction. To do the job well, the savvy exhibit manager will carefully orchestrate both of these elements into one harmonious package with one goal in mind—*results*.

In a nutshell, that's what exhibit management, and this book, are all about.

Exhibit management is a relatively new corporate function. While some organizations have a dedicated exhibit staff, often the role of exhibit management lands on the desk of an unsuspecting, overworked, or unwilling sales or marketing person who feels as if he or she just bought a new car without receiving the ignition key. The car looks good, but it won't take you where you want to go.

Exhibiting is serious business with a real payoff. You will read throughout this book about the value of exhibits in the marketing mix and learn how to realize an accurate, quantifiable return on your exhibiting investment. However, in order to bring about these benefits, there is work involved. This book is your step-by-step guide that will help you get the results you deserve.

Exhibit management is a multitasker's fantasy. There are hundreds of bits and pieces that need to be assembled like a jigsaw puzzle, each interlocking piece carefully fitted into another. Slowly but surely, the whole picture starts to take form. When it's complete, you sit back and enjoy it. Then you take all the pieces apart, put them back in their box, and wait for the next chance to put them together again.

The difference between building a jigsaw puzzle and multitasking is that with the puzzle, you have the luxury of focusing on one piece at a time. When you manage an exhibit program, you are required to juggle many tasks simultaneously. It requires an understanding of face-to-face marketing and the tools to create and implement a plan. The job is not as daunting as it first appears. This book is a methodical guide to creating an exhibit program that produces results.

The planning process starts nine to twelve months before an exhibition. If you give it enough time, you can eliminate the last-minute scramble to get everything done. But for those readers who like the adrenaline rush that comes with producing something as complicated as an exhibit in a few short weeks, let this book become your safety net to ensure that nothing will be overlooked.

As you go through this book, you will learn that your job as an exhibit manager has three key areas: fiscal, physical, and human.

Each of these areas will be examined in detail, giving you the tools you need to be a great exhibit manager. You will learn to create the exhibits that will make you proud of your accomplishments and, more important, produce stellar results for your organization.

Managing the Fiscal Resources

"Give us the tools and we will finish the job."
— Winston Churchill —

Exhibiting Objectives

"Great minds have purposes, others have wishes."
— Washington Irving —

Does this sound familiar? "We're here because we're here, because we're here, because we're here." It's not just the jingle we all sang when the big yellow bus with vinyl seats and a sticky floor pulled into the camp parking lot. It has also become the theme song for 80 percent of all exhibitors at trade shows.

Ask exhibitors why they invest in a trade show and you will hear:

- "We always do this show."
- "We have to be there because our competition is there."
- "My boss thought this might be a good place to be."
- "If we don't go our customers will miss us."
- "We're here because we're here ..."

Investing in a show without setting clear, focused, measurable objectives is like piloting an airplane without a flight plan. Without a focus for all your activities, there is no way to know if you have achieved your goal.

You must establish your objectives before doing anything else. However, it is not as easy as it sounds. You may believe exhibiting does not fall within your marketing activities; you may have conflicting goals among your exhibiting partners; you may have non-sales staff who don't see the value. So, let's walk through the necessary steps to ensure that your next show has a clear focus.

Objectives are the "fundamental strategy of business." Business objectives must be set in all operational areas, including marketing, innovation, human resources, financial resources, physical resources, productivity, social responsibility, and profit requirements.

Your first step is to gain insight into your organization's "basic strategy objective." This term, coined by management guru Peter Drucker in the early 1970s, is still something that organizations have trouble grasping. Your basic strategy objective answers questions such as: Why are we here? Who are we? What is our real purpose? Whether you are examining your purpose personally or corporately, the process is crucial because it examines the core of your being and establishes the logical beginning point of your discussion of objectives.

Some companies look only at profit. Obviously if there is no profit, the very survival of the corporation is at risk. However, an organization that defines itself only in terms of money and return on investment (ROI) is shallow.

Your basic strategy objective goes beyond profit to the very center of your corporate existence. When your business was formed, what purpose did your founders set out for themselves? What motivated them to choose their particular mode of business? Once you understand this, ask yourself if that original focus still has relevance in today's economy.

Here are some recognizable, basic strategy objectives that will assist you in understanding this concept:

- *Mary Kay Cosmetics:* "We reach out to the heart and spirit of women, enabling personal growth and fulfillment for the women whose lives we touch."
- *Walt Disney Corporation:* "To be the world's leading producer and provider of entertainment and information."
- *IBM:* "To be the best service organization in the world."

- *3M:* "To actively contribute to sustainable development through environmental protection, social responsibility, and economic process.
- *McDonalds:* "To be the world's best quick-service restaurant experience."
- *Wal-Mart:* "To deliver quality products at outstanding values."

All of these are examples of highly profitable corporations. In each case, their mission holds a greater purpose. Profit therefore becomes the result.

But, as Drucker explains, these basic strategy objectives are not real objectives. Rather, they are intentions. The dictionary defines intention as "something that somebody plans to do or achieve." Intentions become the rudder that steers a ship through the voyage and a statement that rallies the crew. It is motivational, purposeful, and fulfilling. Without a basic strategy objective, corporations tend to float aimlessly like a ship without a destination.

Setting basic strategy objectives is only the beginning. Unless you take the important next step—setting a clear direction on how to transform intentions into actions—basic strategy objectives will never be achieved. Your marketing plan answers the question, "How do we communicate our intentions to those who will benefit from its message?" You have many traditional choices, including print, television, radio, packaging, direct mail, telemarketing, billboards, flyers, brochures, the Internet, seminars, your sales force, and, of course, exhibitions. Each marketing tool has its strengths and weaknesses. Each must be examined and chosen carefully to ensure that your corporate message reaches its intended audience.

Exhibits hold a special place in the marketing mix. Doug Ducate, CEO of the Centre for Exhibition Industry Research, has referred to exhibitions as "the last vestige of face-to-face marketing." It is important that you choose the tool that gives you the most bang for your buck. While some of these marketing tools are face to face, such as your sales force or seminars, exhibiting is a magnification of the process. At a well-chosen event, you can reach more people in a shorter time than with all the other tools combined. Answer the following questions to determine if exhibiting fits into your marketing plan.

- Why do we want to meet our customers face to face?
- Do we have the resources to do it properly?
- What return do we expect from the exercise?
- How does face-to-face marketing reinforce our overall marketing plan?
- How does our overall marketing plan complement the basic strategy objective?

As a result of answering these questions, you may learn that your exhibit program has more than one objective. At this point it is important to look at each one. You might discover that not all objectives can be satisfied at all shows. In your show selection you may now choose some shows to satisfy objective A and other shows to satisfy objective B. While it's possible to get more than one result from a particular show, with a diversity of visitors attending, the most likely outcome is that you will have to attend different shows to achieve different objectives.

THREE LEVELS OF EXHIBIT OBJECTIVES

As if things were not complicated enough, we now look at exhibiting objectives on three separate levels: corporate, departmental, and individual.

Corporate objectives such as branding, awareness, or image tie the overall marketing plan into a particular show or group of shows. These objectives dictate the overall look and feel of the booth and the message it conveys regardless of the number of internal partners that share the same space. When visitors approach a well-known exhibitor, they recognize the name or brand. Reference to individual departments at this stage can lead to confusion. For example, if you are IBM with forty or fifty different departments, your public knows your word-mark colors, and the look of a typical IBM booth. At first glance, the difference between one department or another is irrelevant. Now here is where you have a delicate balancing act. Your objective at this level is corporate, but it must also be show-specific. While the corporate identity is crucial, it must also answer the question—What is IBM doing at this show?—which brings us to the second level of objectives—departmental objectives.

Each department has its own objectives, which justify their investment in the show. Such objectives are often focused on a specific product, service, or industry need. Whereas IBM has a corporate brand to support, individual departments may be promoting personal computers, property management services, small business solutions, or networking software.

These first two levels of objectives—corporate and departmental—can be found in the following list of 100 reasons to exhibit. As you read through these objectives, identify those that fall into each category for your exhibit program. Ultimately, they fall into two basic categories that are appropriate for your exhibit program—sales and communication.

Sales objectives are those that lead directly to greater profitability. These include increasing sales, gathering qualified leads, and setting appointments. However, some exhibitors decide that sales are not for them and choose a communications objective, such as brand awareness, presence, education, and sampling.

Remember that remaining focused is the secret to successful exhibiting.

100 REASONS FOR EXHIBITING

1. Sell products and services.
2. Gather qualified leads for post-show company follow-up.
3. Introduce new products or services to a market.
4. Demonstrate new products or services.
5. Demonstrate new uses of existing products or services.
6. Give your customers an opportunity to meet the experts.
7. Give your CEO an opportunity to meet your customers.
8. Meet your buyers face to face.
9. Open new markets.
10. See buyers not usually accessible to sales personnel.
11. Find the decision makers.

12. Understand your prospect's decision-making process.
13. Support the decision influencers.
14. Be compared to the competition.
15. Gather competitive intelligence.
16. Solve customers' problems.
17. Obtain feedback on new products.
18. Obtain feedback on existing products.
19. Conduct market research.
20. Find dealers, reps, and agents.
21. Educate dealers, reps, and agents.
22. Find personnel.
23. Educate personnel.
24. Develop leads for dealer, reps, and agents.
25. Reinforce a company image.
26. Establish a new company image.
27. Create a customer database.
28. Support your industry.
29. Highlight new products, services, and initiatives to the media.
30. Reinforce brand awareness.
31. Launch new brand campaign.
32. Distribute product samples.
33. Handle customer complaints.
34. Reinforce your marketing plans.
35. Distribute product or service information.
36. Conduct a sales meeting.
37. Provide networking opportunities.
38. Introduce a new promotion.
39. Introduce a new service.
40. Educate your customers.
41. Introduce new techniques.
42. Reposition your company in a market.
43. Change the perception of your company in a market.
44. Expose new employees to an industry.
45. Learn new industry trends.
46. Network with colleagues.

47. Network with industry professionals.
48. Showcase new products and services.
49. Establish business relationships with international buyers.
50. Introduce your CEO to the media.
51. Support dealers, reps, and agents.
52. Demonstrate your commitment to a market.
53. Demonstrate your commitment to dealers, reps, and agents.
54. Test international buying practices.
55. Influence customer attitudes.
56. Create high ROI opportunities.
57. Uncover technology transfer opportunities.
58. Find new business opportunities.
59. Uncover joint venture opportunities.
60. Unveil licensing opportunities.
61. Find new business location possibilities.
62. Determine the effectiveness of marketing and promotion campaigns.
63. Host special industry hospitality events.
64. Have company experts showcased at seminars and workshops.
65. Market research for future product developments.
66. Introduce new production methods.
67. Use direct influence on decision makers.
68. Build a database.
69. Entertain special customers.
70. Distribute promotional tools.
71. Influence industry trends.
72. Have a portable showroom.
73. Showcase multiple uses for products and services.
74. Interact with a highly targeted audience.
75. Build sales force morale.
76. Give your prospect an opportunity to experience your product/service.
77. Open doors for future sales calls.
78. Achieve immediate sales.
79. Present live product demonstrations.

80. Introduce support services.
81. Offer behind-the-scenes personnel a chance to meet customers.
82. Create a three-dimensional sales presentation.
83. Introduce community awareness initiatives.
84. Support current community awareness initiatives.
85. Find other exhibiting opportunities.
86. Attend educational sessions.
87. Meet with industry spokespersons.
88. Develop new marketing techniques.
89. Demonstrate non-portable equipment.
90. Overcome unfavorable publicity.
91. Publicize company associations with community or industry groups.
92. Explain the effects of corporate changes.
93. Bring senior management closer to customers.
94. Shorten the buying cycle.
95. Train new personnel.
96. Generate excitement for new products/services.
97. Increase corporate profitability.
98. Enhance word-of-mouth markets.
99. Round out the corporate marketing mix.
100. Reach out to customers and communities.

The third level of objectives is individual. Often your booth staff (boothers) will look for opportunities for personal growth. Remember, staff will want to know what's in it for them. There are other ways to get leads or make sales than working at a show. Some staff come to shows feeling resentful about being pulled away from their territories, their regular jobs, or their families. Spending the time to find objectives that help your staff grow as individuals goes a long way toward creating a positive experience for them. Here is a sampling of possible personal objectives:

INDIVIDUAL OBJECTIVES

1. Learn about new technologies.
2. Uncover industry trends.
3. Build a professional network.
4. Introduce yourself and team to industry leaders.
5. Attend industry events.
6. Meet competitors.
7. Develop new people skills.
8. Talk to industry media.
9. Develop camaraderie within departmental teams.
10. Learn more about the scope of the corporation.
11. Talk to customers.
12. Meet organization executives.

You can expand on this list or, better yet, have your staff create their own. Having all three levels of objectives—corporate, departmental, and individual—helps you, the exhibit manager, take the first important step toward creating a successful exhibit program.

GET FOCUSED

Review the list of 100 corporate and departmental objectives and the twelve personal objectives, and identify those that can be applied to your exhibit program. You may find that your list includes a number of objectives in each category. This is a good first step. Now you need to get focused. Having five or ten corporate objectives is a recipe for disaster. You are simply trying to achieve too much with limited time and space. The tighter your focus, the greater your chances of success. Develop a short list of corporate objectives, and then narrow them down further to one or two that will justify the time, expense, and effort that you will invest to mount this display. These corporate objectives also become the engines that drive the basic strategy objective. By reducing your objectives to a precious few, you will focus your energies and resources on your real priorities. With too many objectives, you will run the risk of producing an unfocused, ill-conceived, and awkward attempt that prevents your efforts from delivering the results you want.

By focusing, you will have to make some tough decisions. Leaving out some objectives will be difficult. Sometimes deciding what to leave out can be as difficult as deciding what to include. However, leaving out something does not negate its importance, and the truth is that you may still be able to achieve it another way. Often one objective automatically leads to another. For example, you can create awareness by focusing on new product introduction.

The same argument applies to departmental and personal objectives. Trying to accomplish too much will lead to frustration and disappointment. The more narrow your focus, the better the chance you will have of a successful program.

QUANTIFY YOUR OBJECTIVES

Objectives are of little value unless they are quantified. Here is why quantification is important:

1. *Quantifiable objectives set standards that can be measured.* Later in Chapter 2 you will learn about calculating your return on investment (ROI), but the first step in this process is setting measurable goals. Quantifying is related to the specifics of your show participation. Rather than looking for strictly anecdotal feedback, your information is empirical and comparable from one show to the next.

2. *Quantifiable objectives can be checked periodically.* Rather than waiting for the end of the show to know if you are on the right track, you can adapt your approach along the way to get back on track toward achieving your goal. For example, if your overall show objective is collecting quality leads, you set your goal at fifteen leads per day after determining traffic patterns, attendee habits, etc. If, after the first day, you find that your results fall short of expectations, you have until opening time the next morning to identify the problem and fix it. Perhaps your problem is in your display, or your competitors are out-exhibiting you, or you may have a terrible location, or maybe you just set the wrong objectives in the first place. The challenge is to identify the real

problem and find a solution. This gives you a chance to make the rest of the show profitable and recover from a poor start.

3. *Quantifiable objectives can be divided among your booth staff.* This gives each person a specific target to aim for. At this point each exhibitor needs to ask himself or herself, "How will I know if I have achieved my objectives?"

Be Specific When You Quantify Your Objectives

Sales objectives, such as lead generation or written orders, are relatively easy to quantify. You simply add up your lead cards or sales orders. In contrast, achieving communications objectives presents greater challenges. When measuring the impact of branding, image, or industry support, here is a simple exercise. For example, if your objective is image, ask yourself, "What does image mean? Which three key messages about our image do we want to reinforce with our customers?" This is a great first step.

Let's say that the key messages you identify as part of your company's image are superior service, a helpful staff, and a twenty-four-hour customer hot line. The next question you need to ask is "Who is my target audience?" Rarely will one exhibitor appeal to 100 percent of a show audience. Your audience is specific to you. You must create careful customer profiles that clearly identify your target audience. (See more about creating a customer profile in Chapter 3.) Now you can say to yourself "At the Builder's Show, I want to meet residential builders who have multi-unit projects starting within the next twelve months and tell them about our superior service, helpful staff, and twenty-four-hour customer hot line." See how specific you have become?

Will an increase in sales tell you if your target audience—this group of builders—got the message? Yes, because if they understand what you are all about and if they agree with those messages, they will ultimately buy more from you. But the problem with that is timing. You need to establish objectives that can be measured in the short term—two weeks after the show. Your actual business, depending on your individual sales cycle, could involve months or even years to show results, so the answer is to devise a simple mechanism to gather short-term information such as exit surveys, post-show telephone surveys, increased hits to your web site, and higher traffic for the twenty-four-hour hot line, etc. All these techniques quantify results and tell you definitively whether or not your show was a success.

Yes, you may think, but how does an increase in web traffic relate to more business? The answer will emerge over time. By keeping a statistical tracking system, you will know your success ratios. For example, for every ten qualified leads, how many will lead to business? Two? Three? Five? It is different for everyone. Once you know your success ratios, then the short-term objectives can be equated to long-term profit even if the sale is not yet completed. When it comes to exhibiting, it's important to keep objectives short term.

Be Realistic about Your Objectives

There is no point in reaching for the sky if it is not possible to do so. It can lead to frustration and disappointment. Knowing what is realistic is a matter of educated guesswork. Here is an example:

• Total show attendance: 5,000
• Percentage of attendees who fit into my customer profile: 10 percent or 500
• The average time it takes to talk to one attendee: ten minutes
• Number of active show hours (subtract inactive time such as when conferences are on, downtimes such as late afternoon or early morning, and where you are located in the show): twenty hours

Therefore, boothers should be able to see six visitors per hour over twenty hours, which would equal 120 leads.

But this is not a perfect world, so you will be spending lots of time with visitors who are not qualified. In reality, at this show only one in ten visitors will actually fit your profile. In this example, you may be spending 90 percent of the time (or eighteen hours) talking to unqualified people. This leaves you with a realistic goal of twelve leads. It doesn't sound like much, but in fact it could be very lucrative if indeed they are properly qualified. Remember, I am talking about good leads, not names in a ballot box, but people with whom you had a serious talk during which you gathered some useful information about their situation. These are people you will be following up with after the show is over.

Now ask yourself if there are things you can do in your booth to increase its efficiency. Better signage, pre-show promotions, and sponsorships are worth considering. By adding these additional elements to your plan, you can reduce the 90 percent downtime to perhaps 60 percent or 70 percent, yielding a healthier but realistic target of eighteen to twenty-four leads.

Setting achievable objectives moves you into the select company of exhibitors who exhibit to win. It leaves the 80 percent of exhibitors who don't prepare properly far behind. Setting objectives is the logical beginning for your entire exhibit program. After establishing your objectives, the next step is to get senior management's support by demonstrating how your exhibiting objectives fit in with corporate objectives.

A real obstacle that many managers face is running a trade show program without the full support of their organization. Through lack of understanding or apathy, members of your company may regard trade shows as a necessary evil and not worthy of much more attention. But with management support, the world of possibilities opens; staff are better motivated; cross-promotion opportunities are doable; integration with the overall marketing objectives is assured; senior executives can get into the trenches and participate in the marketing process—you get the picture.

Secure Senior Management Support

What can you do to attain greater commitment from your entire organization? Start at the top with your senior management. If you can show them the rationale of the show plan, how this show fits into the overall goals and objectives of the corporation, and how the show will provide a positive return on investment, a commitment should follow. Trade shows are a marketing exercise. The decision to participate, therefore, needs to complement the corporate marketing objectives. Having a clear handle on these objectives is the first step. Doing a show because you have always done it or because everyone else is there is not real justification. However, understanding that exhibits are an opportunity to meet lots of prospects face to face in a short period gives you a new broader prospective. Think of a marketing objective that can be accomplished at a show. It could be gathering qualified leads, creating a company image, sampling, recruiting, reinforcing relationships, introducing new products, and so on. In fact, there are over 100 realistic and measurable objectives achievable at trade shows.

Now that you have found a justification for the investment, your next job is to develop a rational show plan. Look at the plan from your manager's point of view. Be prepared to tackle some of the following questions.

- What message is my company conveying and how does the trade show involvement help?
- Is there a positive return on my show investment?
- Do I have the resources (human and other) to achieve my trade show goals?
- Who are the attendees we will have a chance to meet at the show?
- How will senior management's commitment enhance my plan?

Add other questions that are relevant to your own situation. Your next job is to find reasonable answers to all these questions and communicate them to the people who need to hear them. If you are doing the show just because someone dumped the file on your desk and you were reluctant to say no, then you can't expect to find much value in the experience for either your company or yourself. However, if you see organizing a show as a tremendous opportunity for personal growth and satisfaction and want to make a real difference in your organization, your chances of success are greatly enhanced. The key to achieving this goal is getting the support of senior management.

Taking on the responsibility of running a show is like running a business for a finite period of time. Like any business, there are costs and rewards. First, convince yourself that this business makes sense and then convince senior management.

IN CONCLUSION

By taking these first crucial steps you are giving your program what it needs to succeed. Without a clear focus and the support of senior management your exhibit marketing program will be mediocre at best. In this day and age, mediocrity just doesn't make the cut.

Budgeting and Financial Management

"Money is like a sixth sense
without which you cannot make a
complete use of the five."
— W. Somerset Maugham —

As an exhibit manager, you have a fiscal responsibility to allocate your resources properly and report results accurately to management. Without money nothing will happen, so the bottom line for your entire exhibit program depends on these next few pages.

The first step is to look at where your budgets come from. Often, they seem to materialize out of thin air. A number magically appears that is available for show and event marketing. Or, the budget is a derivation of the previous year's costs. You spent X dollars last time, so this year you ought to be able to spend X plus or minus 10 percent.

Today you are at ground zero. It is the beginning of a new era in exhibit management for your organization, a time to wipe the slate clean.

A results-oriented, fresh approach is needed. It begins with the measurable, realistic objectives you set in Chapter 1. How much do you need to spend to accomplish these objectives? At this point, it's tough to create a budget based on a wish list. Although you likely will not have the resources to do everything you want, developing a budget based on what you think you need to do the job properly is a good place to start. It forces you to focus on the entire program rather than on one aspect of the plan such as your booth or your promotion. From this you will be able to develop a realistic budget to include resources for all areas of your exhibit.

It's a challenge trying to keep up with escalating costs, new technology, union and show rules, and ever-changing methodologies. The solution is not to create your budget in a vacuum but to get help from suppliers and associations. Have an open dialogue with your suppliers and ask them for price quotes and ballpark estimates based on your objectives. The numbers at this time are "guesstimates," but having an experienced industry person make educated guesses is likely to be a lot closer to reality than if you try do it yourself. Asking for help does not necessarily obligate you in any way. Be up-front with your suppliers. Tell them what you are looking for to create a first draft of your budget, and let them know that there might still be a bidding process before a final vendor is selected.

Another great reference source for putting together a budget is the Trade Show Exhibitors Association (TSEA). In a recent study, it projected the following cost increases from 2003:

PROJECTED EXHIBIT INDUSTRY COST INCREASES FOR 2004	
Exhibit Design and Production	
Audio-visual	1.6%
New production and design	4.6%
Projectionist	.0%
Preparation and refurbishing	3.6%
Photography	−1.3%
Rental and lease	4.8%
Telephone	2.5%
Graphics	3.5%
Utilities (air)	2.8%
Space rental costs	2.8%
Utilities (electric)	1.7%

Freight and Transportation

Utilities (gas)	2.4%
Common carrier	4.3%
Utilities (water)	6.7%
Van lines	0.8%
Drayage	3.2%
Air	3.5%
Carpet	2.7%
Ocean	1.0%

Exhibit-Related Expense

Railway	1.0%
Talent	−1.2%

Show Services

Travel	.0%
Installation and dismantling	3.4%
Lodging	0.1%
Electrical per hour	2.8%
Promotions	5.7%
Electrical per outlet	2.8%
Premiums	0.4%
Plumbing	3.9%
Training	2.9%
Cleaning	1.7%
Lead management	6.4%
Security	3.6%
Floral/plant	1.3%
Furniture	3.5%

Source: TSEA annual budget projections, 2004

It is always helpful to have some past history to determine the increases you might expect. If you are starting from scratch, ballpark numbers will be helpful. *Trade Show Week* proposes two options:

- *Option 1*: Based on the ballpark average for the total cost of a show being three times the cost of exhibit space, if your exhibit space cost $10,000, your total show budget should be $30,000.
- *Option 2*: If you do not know your previous exhibit costs or the actual costs for the shows you are planning, you can base your assumption on square footage. *Trade Show Week* reports that the average square foot cost for exhibits is $21.76. Therefore, if you had rented 200 square feet (18.5 square meters), your costs should be $21.76 × 200 × 3, or $13,056.00.

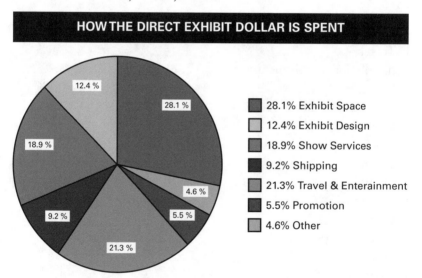

HOW THE DIRECT EXHIBIT DOLLAR IS SPENT

- 28.1% Exhibit Space
- 12.4% Exhibit Design
- 18.9% Show Services
- 9.2% Shipping
- 21.3% Travel & Enterainment
- 5.5% Promotion
- 4.6% Other

Source: CEIR SM22 *The Power of Exhibitions*

How Do You Compare?

Averages are interesting to look at, but they are just averages. No two situations are alike. Use the figure above to give yourself some direction as to the overall weighting of your show budget, but realize that your individual situation may vary from the norm.

CALCULATE THE AMOUNT OF
EXHIBIT SPACE REQUIRED

The Centre for Exhibition Research reports that "the larger the exhibit, the better the chance of visitors remembering it." However, not all trade show exhibitors have the luxury of size.

In some cases it can make the overall costs of exhibiting prohibitive, or additional space is not always available. And in most cases it simply is not necessary. Exhibitors can easily make up for lack of space by creating innovative and exciting activities such as demonstrations, entertainment, or sponsorships. The simple solution is to calculate the ideal amount of space you should have; then if there are budget or other constraints that prevent you from having what you need to achieve your objectives, add in other enhancements to make up for what you don't have in the amount of space.

The first step begins with your objective. In Chapter 3 you will learn how to establish a customer profile. It is crucial to stay focused. If you aim to reach 100 percent of the visitors (which exhibitors only rarely do), then you are spreading your resources too thin. As a result, you will likely neglect some wonderful opportunities. For example, let's say the show has a projected audience of 20,000 people. After talking to show management or reviewing the audited information from previous shows, you determine that 8 percent of this audience fit your profile. The math looks like this:

$$20,000 \times 8\% = 1,600 \text{ visitors}$$

Will all of these 1,600 people stop by your booth? The answer is often no. Every show is different. The number of visitors who actually stop at each exhibit varies. The Audience Interest Factor (AIF) calculates the number of highly interested people. If you don't know your AIF, the rule of thumb is 45 percent. If you keep track of your show results, then over time you will learn your specific AIF. For now, use the 45 percent rule of thumb, so the potential number of visitors is:

$$1,600 \times 45\% = 720 \text{ potential visitors}$$

Now, you know that you need enough space to accommodate 720 visitors over the course of the show. Two additional bits of information will be very helpful: How long will it take you to accomplish your goal with each visitor? And how long is the show?

Measure the length of the show in terms of active show hours rather than total hours. Every show will produce a different flow of traffic. Often there are distractions such as a conference or workshops where all delegates are drawn off the show floor to attend education sessions, hear a keynote speaker, or watch a floor show. At some shows, more people arrive in the late afternoon than early morning. There are many variables and it's important to be aware of as many of them as possible. For our purposes, let's say that the show is open for eight hours each day for three days, which means there will be twenty-four show hours. You have determined that the last two hours of each day and one hour during lunch are slow, so your calculations of active hours will be:

$$24 \text{ show hours} - 9 \text{ (3 slow hours} \times 3 \text{ days)} = 15 \text{ active show hours}$$

Now divide the number of visitors by the number of active hours:

$$720 \div 15 = 48 \text{ visitors per hour}$$

The next step is to calculate the human element. How long do your staff have to spend with each visitor in order to accomplish their goal? Let's assume it is ten minutes. This is a rough estimate since each person they meet will not necessarily fit your profile. You will spend time with unqualified people, time standing around, and so on, so factor in unproductive time in your equation. For example, let's set a target for each booth person to talk to six people per hour. If we have the potential of forty-eight visitors per hour, then in our example we need 8 booth people.

Another rule of thumb states that each booth person needs 50 square feet (4.5 square meters) of unoccupied space to work in. This means that in a 10-foot by 10-foot (3-meter by 3-meter) booth, two people can carry on two conversations simultaneously with two visitors.

The key word here is "unoccupied." You need to include your product, displays, demonstrations, furniture, and so on. In our example, we would need 500 square feet (46 square meters) of space (eight booth people plus 100 square feet/9.3 square meters for product display).

BOOTH SPACE CALCULATION

Total number of potential visitors	_____
Percentage that represents target	_____
Total number of targeted visitors	_____
AIF	_____
Net potential booth visitors	_____ (a)
Number of show hours	_____
less inactive hours	_____
Active show hours	_____ (b)
Number of visitors per hour (a ÷ b)	_____ (c)
Amount of time spent with each visitor	_____ (d)
Number of visitors per hour (d ÷ 60)	_____ (e)
Number of boothers (e ÷ c)	_____ (f)
Amount of booth space (f × 50 square feet + amount of space for hardware, furniture, products, etc.)	_____

Now, armed with numbers, you can begin creating your first draft budget.

EXHIBIT COST SUMMARY

Cost Description	Estimate	Actual	Subtotals
Display			
Design and detailing	$_____	$_____	
Refurbishing	$_____	$_____	
Crates and packing	$_____	$_____	
Furnishings	$_____	$_____	
Install and dismantle	$_____	$_____	
Storage	$_____	$_____	
			$_____

Cost Description	Estimate	Actual	Subtotals
Transportation			
Carrier	$_____	$_____	
Customs	$_____	$_____	
Export licence	$_____	$_____	
Drayage	$_____	$_____	
			$_____
Labor			
Electrician	$_____	$_____	
Carpenter	$_____	$_____	
Painters	$_____	$_____	
Plumbers	$_____	$_____	
Riggers	$_____	$_____	
Unskilled labor	$_____	$_____	
Machine operators	$_____	$_____	
Florist	$_____	$_____	
Security	$_____	$_____	
			$_____
Promotion			
Advertising	$_____	$_____	
Mailings	$_____	$_____	
Printing	$_____	$_____	
Postage/courier	$_____	$_____	
Sponsorships	$_____	$_____	
Premiums	$_____	$_____	
Talent	$_____	$_____	
Hotel (talent)	$_____	$_____	
Travel (talent)	$_____	$_____	
Literature	$_____	$_____	
Web site development	$_____	$_____	
Web site updates	$_____	$_____	
			$_____

Cost Description	Estimate	Actual	Subtotals
Product samples	$ _____	$ _____	
Prizes	$ _____	$ _____	
On-site			
(billboards, marquees, etc.)	$ _____	$ _____	
			$ _____
Show services			
Utilities	$ _____	$ _____	
Space rental	$ _____	$ _____	
Furniture/carpet rental	$ _____	$ _____	
Badges	$ _____	$ _____	
Cleaning	$ _____	$ _____	
Lead-retrieval system rental	$ _____	$ _____	
Demonstration equipment	$ _____	$ _____	
Hospitality	$ _____	$ _____	
Telephone	$ _____	$ _____	
Internet hookup	$ _____	$ _____	
			$ _____
Booth staff			
Per diem allowance	$ _____	$ _____	
Hotel	$ _____	$ _____	
Travel	$ _____	$ _____	
Ground transportation	$ _____	$ _____	
Group entertainment	$ _____	$ _____	
Staff training	$ _____	$ _____	
Outside research	$ _____	$ _____	
			$ _____
Total exhibit cost			$ _____

Objective _____

Cost per unit (the total exhibit cost divided by the
number of units in your objective; that is, the number
of leads, image impressions, web site hits, increase
in traffic, and so on.) $ _____

Your first draft was a wish list. Now it's time to look at reality. In a perfect world, this represented all you needed. It was an important step because it gave you a chance to create a perfect exhibit plan on paper before you tried to do it for real. It enabled you to give proper attention to all the details of your exhibit planning rather than make the mistake of allocating too much to one area while ignoring others completely. The reality, however, is that you don't have an unlimited budget. Before you request more money from management, you have to earn that privilege through success. Once you have proven that good exhibit planning creates positive results, obtaining increases to your exhibit budget should become easier.

If your wish list required an investment of $10,000 and you have only $5,000, you will have to eliminate 50 percent of your plans. The advantage of creating a wish list first gives you an opportunity to tweak your budget properly by examining each expense category, grouping cost-saving opportunities rather than eliminating an entire category.

To compound the challenge, you may have different corporate partners who have their own agenda involved in your exhibit. What may be a frill to one department may be a necessity to another. Similar to any other budgeting exercise, you will have to balance many needs. Find out what each partner wants and what they need. You may have to do this through a series of meetings. If you find that one partner must have something that other partners do not need, then you have justification for charging back a larger proportion of the cost to that partner's budget. You should begin budgeting at least one year in advance since it may take some time to reach a final agreement.

Here are some typical examples of where exhibitors have managed to save budget dollars.

Display

First-time exhibitors may consider renting booth hardware before taking the plunge and committing to one system. Typical rental costs are about 20 percent of the retail value of the hardware, excluding signs and graphics. Another consideration is refurbishing an older booth rather than replacing it. If the structure is in good shape, then re-facing it can be cost effective.

If you are a new exhibitor looking to purchase your first booth, consider buying a used one or renting. Check with your display house for a good lead or look on one of the Internet resale sites such as *www.eBay.com.*

Transportation

Generally shows have an official freight forwarder. At first glance, it may seem more expensive, but the official freight forwarder will likely guarantee on-time delivery because it understands the show and often gets priority at the loading docks. Whenever possible, avoid last-minute shipments because charges can be exorbitant. If your event does not have a designated freight forwarder, consider forming a group with other exhibitors from your area to negotiate better rates collectively.

The cost of drayage—moving goods from the show's receiving dock to your show floor space—is a reality in many exhibit facilities. Depending on the location, you may be able to move some things yourself, such as a booth that comes in a case on wheels, but before you move anything, check the local labor rules. Drayage is usually calculated on a cost per hundred weight basis (CWT). This means that if your shipment weighs 510 pounds (231 kilograms), you will be charged for 600 pounds (272 kilograms).

Labor

In certain jurisdictions you can provide your own labor, while in others you cannot. Be sure to read the show rules carefully. On-site labor charges can be minimized by ensuring that your display needs as little work as possible on-site. A pre-show checkup will eliminate a lot of last-minute structural problems.

Promotion

Planning early for the entire year is an easy way to stretch your promotion budget. It gives you the cost advantage of multiple-unit purchasing of advertising space, lower per-unit costs on premiums and printed material, as well as an opportunity to work collectively with other exhibitors.

Ensure that your boothers limit the use of give-away items to serious visitors only. Brochures, premiums, and other trade show tools are wasted when exhibit staff give them away rather than pack them up and ship them home for the next show.

Other exhibitors often welcome the idea of cross-promotion. You can trade products or place promotional materials in each other's booth with a sign acknowledging where the attendee can learn more about a particular product. For example, if you sell computer hardware, find someone else at the show who sells computer furniture. If you sell flowers, find someone else who sells vases. You can also put links on each other's web sites, conduct joint advertising programs, and participate in collective promotional techniques such as the use of a passport at the event. A passport is a card that each visitor must take to designated booths to be authorized. Once the passport pages have all been stamped, the visitor enters it into a draw for a prize. Often the show manager will organize this, but if he or she doesn't, you can get together with five or six other exhibitors and do it yourself.

The Media

If you cultivate your relationship carefully with members of the media, they can be terrific promotional partners. There is no guarantee that you will get what you want, but there is little cost and the potential reward, such as moving to the front of the line when it's time for editorial coverage, is so high that it is worth the effort.

Show Services

The cost difference between ordering services within the show deadlines and at the last minute is substantial. Read your show manual carefully and ensure that you have ordered everything on time.

Land-line telephones are expensive to install and often redundant since most of your staff have their own cell phones or PDAs. Unless you need the land line for an Internet connection, this is one expense you can avoid.

Booth Staff

In some locations you can hire professional booth staff from a local agency rather than bringing your own. Often the cost of travel, accommodation, and the time away from the office makes bringing staff uneconomical. However, don't forget that if you hire temporary people, they will need some training, so plan to hire them the day before and make it a training day.

THE FINAL BUDGET

After you have done your homework, trimmed the budget, and worked with your internal partners, you are ready to finalize your exhibit budget. Remember, your exhibit budget is your chance to develop a workable plan on paper before committing real resources. Compare your costs to your potential short-term income. Actual sales increases take time. Evaluating the event in the short term is the only practical way of measuring success. Here's where history can be a great teacher. Record previous results, post-event briefings, lead history, comments, and notes for future events. The files will include individual events plus a summary of your entire exhibit program. This way anyone who is planning an exhibit has the benefit of earlier lessons. You need to record your results on a show-by-show basis.

Completing the Budget

From your final estimated budget, you need to look at your actual costs. This requires collecting invoices from suppliers and expense reports from your staff. Even if these invoices go to another department for processing, it is crucial that you see them first. You need this information as quickly as possible.

Your budget also included revenue, as explained in your objective. These numbers should be easily accessible. Start collecting information on the number of leads, image impressions, conversations with visitors, post-show surveys, increases in booth traffic, or post-show web site hits. With this information in hand, you can now complete the budget and add up the totals.

Establishing Your Return on Investment

There are several methods of measuring the exhibit ROI:

1. *Percentage increase in booth activity from previous show*: Many experienced exhibitors calculate ROI by dividing the actual numbers from this year's show by the previous year's figures, multiplying by 100. For example, if this year's number is 178 and last year's was 132, then $178 \div 132 = 1.348 \times 100 = 134$ or a 34 percent increase. The figures could indicate direct sales, qualified leads, attendance at in-booth activities, or inquiries.

    For example, if your last show cost $10,000 and you obtained 100 quality leads, then your cost per lead is $100.00. If you spent that same $10,000 at the next show, you could reasonably expect to receive similar results.

    However, you should be looking at some improvement. Will each new lead cost an additional $100.00 to get? Probably not, since you can take advantage of economies of scale. You might say that next year you want to get 200 leads and will invest $15,000. You can spend the extra budget on better booth hardware, increased promotion, new offerings, etc. Your average lead cost has now dropped to $75.00. It is relatively easy to measure this at the end of the show and see if you reached your target.

2. *The number of existing or new prospects actually stopping by the booth*: Booth traffic is a reasonable way to measure your ROI, but not just any traffic—it must be the right traffic.

    It's no achievement to create a booth that will attract every visitor that passes by. The real challenge is creating a booth that attracts the *right* visitors—the ones you targeted before the show began. Only a select few exhibitors want to talk to everyone. It is crucial that each boother understands what types of visitors are targeted and has the skills to assess people quickly to see if they fit the profile. Tracking them is another way of measuring ROI.

3. *Increase in post-show activities*: Another approach is to measure an increase in post-show activities such as web hits, office drop-ins, or telephone inquiries. Often show visitors are offered an incentive, such as a prize for entering a contest on-line or a time-sensitive coupon. This enables you to make post-show inquiries so you can track success. A simple increase in activity immediately following the exhibition can serve as a measurement of success.

4. *Number of qualified leads*: Qualified leads are visitors whom your staff has taken the time to talk to or those who have expressed some level of interest in your product or service. These are collected on lead cards or lead-retrieval systems provided by show management (see Chapter 11).

5. *Survey results*: Surveying visitors to ensure that they understood the information provided at the booth and that the booth staff were on the right course is a useful method of testing communication objectives. Exhibit or post-show surveys are a great way of confirming that this information was properly understood.

6. *Media exposure*: Seeing concrete results from your first meeting with the media often takes time. Therefore, you are better off using short-term measurements. A list of the media people you've met and/or the activities you engaged in with them can be a source of measurement. However, building media relationships is more than a handshake at a reception. It involves attracting them to visit your booth or engaging them in a detailed discussion about your products or services. The number of media kits distributed in the media room is not a valid measurement on its own, although high media demand for your kits is usually a good sign.

7. *Other measures*: The list goes on and on. This short list is only a beginning. The discussion of methods of measurement goes back to the discussion of setting objectives in Chapter 1. If you have

thought out the process clearly, you will be able to measure your success. Use your imagination!

Compare Your Results

After you have calculated your actual costs and rewards, it's time to compare. The raw numbers will let you know if this venture was on target, but astute exhibit managers need to know how this event compared with others, what did they right, and what they could improve. Using raw numbers, you can determine such things as the cost per qualified lead, per media contact, or per web site hit. A comparison chart can provide a helpful summary:

COMPARATIVE MARKETING RESULTS						
Objective	*Trade Show A*	*ABC Magazine*	*WKFM Radio*	*Direct Mail Campaign*	*Fax/ Email Blast*	*Other*
Cost per unit	$	$	$	$	$	$
Image	$	$	$	$	$	$
Leads	$	$	$	$	$	$
Media	$	$	$	$	$	$
Sales	$	$	$	$	$	$
Meeting dealers	$	$	$	$	$	$
Other	$	$	$	$	$	$

The next step is to ensure you are comparing apples to apples. If your objective was to obtain a certain number of leads, did you get the same quality leads from each of the various marketing tools? Was the quality of the media contact greater because you had a chance to meet face to face? Did attendees remember more details about your product and service because they had a chance to see and feel it on the show floor, or did they remember just as much regardless of where they first heard about your product or service? These are important questions that often cannot be answered in the short term, but with your show files in place, over time you will be able to use real results to evaluate the effectiveness of your efforts to reach your objectives. This is the acid test for measuring the value of your exhibit.

With some history to draw on, you will be able to complete forms such as the following.

LEAD HISTORY				
	Two Years Ago	*Last Year*	*Current Year*	*Average*
Number of leads	560	840	1,230	877
Number of shows	3	4	5	
Average lead/show	187	210	246	219
Cost per lead	$390.00	$310.00	$275.00	$325.00

What's Next?

At this point you have a clear understanding of the costs of the exhibit program and how it compares to other marketing efforts, but you need to know what to do next. Meeting an objective may be a result of savvy marketing or because you set the bar too low. Missing an objective may be the result of some hidden mistake that, if corrected, could produce a spectacular show. This is a good time to get some help from your trade show team.

Within two weeks of the event, have each member of your team complete the following form. Encourage them to be honest with their responses, and don't get defensive when you read their answers.

POST-SHOW EVALUATION FORM

Name of Exhibit: _____

Date: _____

Part 1:

Please rate the following on a scale from 1 to 5, with 1 being very poor and 5 being excellent.

Ranking	1	2	3	4	5
Pre-show promotion	1	2	3	4	5
Location	1	2	3	4	5
Show hours	1	2	3	4	5
Booth scheduling	1	2	3	4	5
Booth size	1	2	3	4	5
Design	1	2	3	4	5
Graphics	1	2	3	4	5
Technical support	1	2	3	4	5
Lead collecting	1	2	3	4	5
In-booth demonstrations	1	2	3	4	5
Product mix	1	2	3	4	5
Premiums	1	2	3	4	5
Draws	1	2	3	4	5
Hospitality	1	2	3	4	5
Our staff's presence	1	2	3	4	5
Our staff's professionalism	1	2	3	4	5
Staffing schedule	1	2	3	4	5
Quality of visitors	1	2	3	4	5
Competitor's display	1	2	3	4	5
Show management	1	2	3	4	5
Show amenities	1	2	3	4	5
Overall show program	1	2	3	4	5

Part 2:

Add additional comments on any of the above that will be helpful in our future planning.

In the future, do you think this event is worth participating?

☐ Yes ☐ No

Why? _____
_____
_____
_____

What changes would you make? _____
_____
_____
_____
_____

Do you know of other events that we should explore?

☐ Yes ☐ No

If yes, where? _____
_____
_____
_____

Add any additional comments that will be helpful in evaluating our future presence at this event. _____
_____
_____
_____
_____

The first part of this form deals with perceptions. Don't feel limited by the categories on this form. Add as many questions as required to get the information you need. Once you have collected all the feedback sheets from your team, you will be able to detect some emerging patterns.

Part 2 of the form is more subjective. This will include personal reactions, comments, and hearsay that, when examined in the light of day, will provide important clues for evaluating your future plans.

FINANCIAL MANAGEMENT

The next step is to summarize information so that anyone picking up the file gets a snapshot of the show, can compare how it stacks up against others, and can review the total results of your entire event marketing program.

Show by Show

The exhibit summary below is a sample report that will give future exhibit managers a thumbnail sketch of the event and your recommendations. It starts with an event description and your overall rating, followed by a line-by-line review of the show. It is a great chance for you to tally the results of your team's post-show surveys as well as your own observations. The report also includes information about what you would keep or change if you were to do this show again in the future. If the show results in a poor line-by-line summary, it is still helpful because there is still much to learn even from an unsuccessful event.

EXHIBIT SUMMARY: SHOW BY SHOW
Show: _____
Location: _____
Date: _____
Exhibit manager: _____
Departments involved: _____
Exhibit objective: _____
Theme of the event: _____
Number of attendees: _____

Number of exhibitors:

Overall rating of this event: Excellent   Fair   Poor

Item	*Actual Cost*	*Recommendations*

Display

Design and detailing	$ _____	_____
Refurbishing	$ _____	_____
Crates and packing	$ _____	_____
Furnishings	$ _____	_____
Install and dismantle	$ _____	_____
Storage	$ _____	_____

Transportation

Carrier	$ _____	_____
Customs	$ _____	_____
Export licence	$ _____	_____
Drayage	$ _____	_____

Labor

Electrician	$ _____	_____
Carpenter	$ _____	_____
Painters	$ _____	_____
Plumbers	$ _____	_____
Riggers	$ _____	_____
Unskilled labor	$ _____	_____
Machine operators	$ _____	_____
Florist	$ _____	_____
Security	$ _____	_____

Promotion

Advertising	$ _____	_____
Mailings	$ _____	_____
Printing	$ _____	_____

continued

Item	Actual Cost	Recommendations
Postage/courier	$_____	_____
Sponsorships	$_____	_____
Premiums	$_____	_____
Talent	$_____	_____
Hotel (talent)	$_____	_____
Travel (talent)	$_____	_____
Literature	$_____	_____
Product samples	$_____	_____
Prizes	$_____	_____
On-site (billboards, marquees, etc.)	$_____	_____
Show services		
Utilities	$_____	_____
Space rental	$_____	_____
Furniture/carpet rental	$_____	_____
Badges	$_____	_____
Demonstration equipment	$_____	_____
Hospitality	$_____	_____
Telephone	$_____	_____
Booth staff		
Per diem allowance	$_____	_____
Hotel	$_____	_____
Travel	$_____	_____
Ground transportation	$_____	_____
Group entertainment	$_____	_____
Staff training	$_____	_____
Outside research	$_____	_____
Total exhibit cost	$_____	

Summary: _____

Objective: _____

Cost per unit (the total exhibit cost divided by the number of units in your objective) $ _____

Overall observations and recommendations:

Show-by-Show Comparison

You will want to know whether or not each show achieved your objectives and what was the cost involved in each. You should prepare a separate summary for each type of event, i.e., one for trade shows, one for truck shows (a traveling event that is housed in a truck, van, or other motorized vehicle), one for stand-alone events, etc. This ensures that you are comparing apples to apples. It lets you know which shows worked and which didn't. It is also helpful when you are setting your targets for the next year's program. The chart will look something like the following.

SHOW-BY-SHOW COMPARISON					
Show	*Location*	*Leads*	*Cost/Lead*	*Rating*	*Comments*
Machine	Chicago	385	$290	Excellent	Need a larger exhibit
Tool and die	Atlanta	132	$459	Poor	Attendee quality poor
Truck	Toronto	260	$285	Excellent	Good facility and well-run show
OEM	New York	385	$259	Excellent	Good traffic and mix of exhibitors
Manufacturing	Seattle	67	$1,090	Poor	Little interest in our products

EXHIBIT ANNUAL REPORT

Most annual reports are based on past history. The exhibit annual report, while also based on past history, takes into account the future as well. Preparing the exhibit annual report is an opportunity to look at each exhibit in detail, summarize the results, and create a record of your entire exhibit program. Throughout the year as each event wraps up, record your actual results and include this information in your annual exhibit report. Your annual report is an excellent way of ending one cycle and beginning the next. Based on this information, you will make fewer mistakes, fix what went wrong, capitalize on your strengths, set better objectives, and be in a stronger position to request increases for your exhibiting budget.

Now that you have looked at each type of exhibiting event in your marketing plan, it is time to create your annual exhibit report. This is a more comprehensive report that includes a financial summary as well as notes about the events, people, and hardware that made the show program possible. Preparing such a comprehensive report once a year is often enough. This is a very helpful tool for budget purposes as well as an opportunity to evaluate the overall effectiveness of your exhibit program. It gives you the big picture that so often gets lost in the details of planning and organizing exhibits. Your plan started with a big picture and it should end that way as well.

Your annual report may look something like the following.

> **B & B WIDGET MANUFACTURING COMPANY**
> **EXHIBIT ANNUAL REPORT**
>
> ## Summary
> Last year the exhibit program was able to produce excellent results. Overall we were able to generate 2,019 good quality leads and introduce our products in fourteen new markets, increasing the awareness of B & B from 5 percent to 46 percent. We exhibited at five trade shows, twelve hospitality events, and conducted three regional seminars. Our total cost was $504,750.00, which breaks down to a cost per lead of $250.00, an 11 percent reduction from last year's figure of $275.00.

The Event Programs

Trade Shows
The five shows were industry based and held in various cities across the U.S. and Canada. Two of the five were poor and we do not recommend attending them again. We have identified two new show opportunities in Dallas and Los Angeles that are worth adding to next year's plan. The three remaining shows proved to be excellent. At each show we had 400 square feet (37 square meters) of exhibit space using our existing hardware, supplemented by new signs and graphics. Next year we will use the same hardware, except for Chicago where we will obtain additional space and supplement our exhibiting hardware with a rental product.

Hospitality Events
The twelve hospitality events were held in conjunction with existing industry events around North America. There were four golf tournaments, three luncheons, and five client appreciation nights in conjunction with our trade show program. Total attendance at these events was 5,016 people. At each event we were able to display the corporate sign and banners. A post-event survey indicated an overall 38 percent increase in awareness of B & B as a major sector supplier. We hired an outside event management firm to handle the logistics. It is recommended that because of the wide geographic reach and the limited number of internal staff, outsourcing would be a good investment.

Seminars
Three regional seminars were held. All were targeted at the plant engineers. This initiative was designed to make B & B top of mind to these important influencers of decisions. Our survey showed that plant engineers experienced some confusion in the marketplace between our products and those of our major competitor. Rather than trying to explain the differences to individual visitors, we decided to conduct information seminars. At the

continued

three events we attracted a total of 183 plant engineers of whom thirty-five were current B & B customers. During each event engineers were able to hear from our senior product development specialist and network with other engineers. As a result of these seminars, we have obtained forty-seven individual appointments to discuss our solutions further.

SUMMARY OF RESULTS

Event	Number	Cost	Results	Cost Per Objective	Audience Interest Factor
Trade shows	5	$504,750	2,019 leads	$250.00 per lead	
Hospitality	12	$75,240	5,016 attendees	38% increase in awareness = $15.00 per contact	
Seminars	3	$18,725	183 attendees, 47 appointments	Cost per appointment = $398.40	
Total	20	$598,715			

Long-Term Implications

Based on results from prior years, the following are the long-term implications of our exhibit program.

Leads

In the past we have been able to close one in four quality leads within one year of obtaining that lead. The average opening order is $4,800.00. Therefore, the new leads should generate an additional $2,424,000.00.

> 2,019 leads
>
> 25 percent convert to business in twelve months = 505
>
> Average opening order = $4,800.00
>
> Additional income = $2,424,000.00

Awareness

For each percentage point rise in awareness (38 percent), our business increases by $2,300.00, so we can look forward to an additional $87,400.00

Appointments

Appointments with plant managers based on past experience has led to a one-in-two closing rate with an average opening order of $4,800.00 × 23 = $110,400.00.

Objective	Number	History	Revenue/Unit	Total Revenue	Cost
Leads	2,019	1 in 4	$4,800 opening order	$2,424,000	$504,750
Awareness	38%		1% = $2,300	$87,400	$75,240
Appointments	47	1 in 2	$4,800 opening order	$110,400	$18,725
Total				$2,621,800	$598,715

Our acquisition cost for new business is 22.8 percent in the first year.

The Future

In the future we will continue with these three marketing efforts. We will put a greater effort into our trade show presence at larger shows and maximize our presence by combining our seminar, trade show, and hospitality plans at a few smaller regional events. Next year we will also increase our staff training to further increase our return at each event. We will also implement a study to determine the long-range implications for our marketing plans beyond the one-year mark.

In addition, in conjunction with the company's desire to expand into international markets, we will begin to explore the various exhibit-marketing opportunities in specific countries and regions.

IN CONCLUSION

This entire book comes down to finances. There is no point in planning if you do not have the resources to implement that plan. Too many exhibitors fail because they bite off more than they can chew. By taking a methodical approach as outlined in this chapter, you will be able to approach your exhibit plans with the confidence and the knowledge that you have both fiscal and moral support behind you. Your exhibit annual report becomes the recorded legacy of your exhibit program.

Choosing the Right Event

"There is a tide in the affairs of men,
Which, taken at the flood, leads on to fortune."
— William Shakespeare —

I once asked a show manager to tell me the most important criteria an exhibitor should consider when choosing a show. "Simple," he said without hesitation, "it comes down to three things—audience, audience, and audience." Admittedly, understanding the audience may be a key factor in finding the right audience for you, but it is not as simple as it sounds. This chapter is a step-by-step guide to determining the best places for you to exhibit.

UNDERSTAND YOUR OBJECTIVES

Everything starts at the same place—with your objectives. Understanding your objectives will influence your choices. Each objective may require a different audience to meet different needs (see Chapter 1).

DEFINE YOUR AUDIENCE

Who do you want to attract to your exhibit? If your answer is "Anyone with a pulse and a wallet," your response is misleading. Rarely will one product or service be appropriate for everyone. Even if they could use your product or service, there is no certainty that they would be in a position to make a decision. Trying to be everything to everyone is a mistake. We have moved from a nation of generalists casting a broad net to catch whatever we can to a nation of specialists—specialty stores, television, or even specialty chat rooms. Casting a wide net is what Internet spammers do. They buy lists with millions of names for low prices with the rationale that if they can score one or two hits, the cost-versus-results ratio makes sense. Exhibiting is different. You don't have the luxury of hiding in cyberspace. You are meeting customers face to face and casting that broad net makes no sense. Furthermore, when you exhibit, the cost per contact is much higher, so you need to ensure that the quality of hits is as high as possible. Your most effective marketing strategy is to target relevant messages to those who are most receptive.

ESTABLISH A CUSTOMER PROFILE

The solution is to create customer profiles. There are sophisticated tools at your disposal such as cluster analysis, factor analysis, or latent class analysis, but good profiles can be created with some simple foresight, planning, and a dash of common sense. There are two kinds of customer profiles. The first is demographic—an analysis of individuals or businesses based on factors such as age, spending habits, location, type of business, etc. The second is psychographic—based on how customers react in certain situations, such as how often they order a particular product, what they order, when they order, what marketing stimuli they respond to most positively, and so on. Both types of analysis are helpful, so let's create a meaningful customer profile that includes both demographic and psychographic considerations.

The best place to start is with existing customers. This first step gives you an understanding of why they buy your product or service. Participation in a commercial exchange is not what defines a customer. Defining a customer starts with a basic understanding of how a customer perceives the features and benefits of what you have to offer.

Talking in terms of benefits is crucial for your customer profiling. There is an old saying in sales training that "people buy solutions."

Most customers approach you looking for specific solutions to their problems or needs. Once you thoroughly understand those needs, the next step is to offer a solution. In some cases it is a simple matter. You hand the customer a package of computer paper that he requested and tell him how much it will cost. Or, you swipe the debit card, print out a receipt, get a signature, and that's that, but not all transactions are that simple. You may have to describe a product or service or proposal. You may have to convey background information to help the customer make choices. This is where many boothers run into trouble. They fail to communicate their solutions effectively.

Features are what a product is. Take the example of a simple coffee cup. Upon examination, we can see that the cup is a hollow cylinder with a closed, flat bottom, an open top, and a handle on the side. This particular cup holds 8 ounces (250 milliliters) and is decorated with a particular pattern. These are all features. They are interesting, but a customer might say "So what?" Marketers are constantly telling us about features such as a 25-megahertz clock speed, dual carburetors, or longer pharmacokinetic half-life. What they are not telling us in these statements is how the product or service meets our need.

Back to the coffee cup. The flat bottom is designed so the cup will sit on a table and the contents won't pour on our lap. The handle allows us to hold a hot cup of coffee without burning our fingers. The design on the side makes the cup attractive to serve to company. The size makes for a hefty whack of caffeine first thing in the morning. To a customer who has never seen a coffee cup before and is looking for some vessel for drinking coffee, these benefit statements would be helpful.

A 25-megahertz clock speed indicates that the computer will operate faster than most other machines on the market. Dual carburetors mean a more responsive engine. Longer pharmacokinetic half-life means the patient will have to take the medicine only once a day. Now we are talking in terms that the customer can relate to.

However, all customers are different. Let's go back to the coffee cup. What differentiates your coffee cup from others on the market? Surely they all have flat bottoms, handles, and sizes that include an 8-ounce (250-milliliter) variety, so what is so special about your coffee cup? Maybe it is the design, the price, the convenience, and so on. Why do your customers buy your products? It is important to know this to target future marketing efforts.

Talking in terms of benefits puts you in your customers' position. It enables you to think about your offering in their terms. When you understand how your existing customers benefit from your products and services, you gain powerful insights into how future customers will gain similar benefits. You can do the following exercise on individual products or by grouping similar products and services together. The first step in profiling is to examine your products, services, and programs through your customers' eyes as follows.

Product	Features	Benefits	Most Likely Customer(s)

FOCUS ON YOUR MARKET

Rarely (but not always) will you have a product or service that appeals to 100 percent of an audience. Be careful about over generalizing your message. Some exhibitors assume that because they are the only game in town, everyone is interested in their message. Let's examine the example of an agency that promotes healthy living. It may believe that its message is for everyone. True, while everyone may benefit, not everyone will care. Some people pay only lip service to a healthy diet. Exhibitors will be misusing trade shows if they believe that simply by reaching these people, they will remember the message—that is, the next time they're out for dinner, they will think twice about asking for the extra order of fries with gravy. There are certain people who are very interested in improving their eating habits and who need your vital information to make good choices. Your job is simply to find the people whom you can best help and then help them. Getting focused is the process of breaking down a large group into smaller segments with specific characteristics. This is done by studying demographic, psychographic, behavioral, and causation data.

Demographics answer the question, "Who is my customer?" It is an analysis of all the pertinent data that defines the characteristics of your customer. Demographics enable you to segment your overall customer base into helpful categories.

In a business-to-customer example, you may define your customer demographics in the following terms: age, income, gender, geography, profession, education, wealth, family makeup, nationality, homeowner/renter, etc. For a business-to-business focus demographics, the qualifiers may include: size of company, type of products sold, revenue, budget, number of employees, number of branches, ownership, industry, industry sector, age, and so on.

Psychographics answer the question, "What do they do?" This is a chance to examine your target audience's attitudes, beliefs, and emotions. The following are samples of psychographic variables in the business-to-consumer marketplace: family stage, hobbies, status awareness, outside interests, leisure time, social responsibility, lifestyle, charitable affiliations, etc. In the business-to-business marketplace, psychographic elements include: social responsibility, environmental conscience, business style, position within an industry, innovations, affiliations, employee relations, workforce type, management style, employee remuneration, shareholder relations, and so on. By adding psychographics to the demographic information, you increase the richness of your customer understanding.

Behavioral inquiries answer the question "How do they do it?" This is an in-depth look at customer demographics and psychographics in action. Whether you are in a business-to-customer or business-to-business marketplace, you can analyze your customers according to their habits in terms of the number of times they purchase, how often, the amount of product purchased, the decision-making cycle, and where the purchase was made.

Causation analysis answers the question, "Why do they do what they do?" Causation is the sum total of all the demographic, psychographic, and behavioral data you have accumulated. It matches up your features and benefits with your customers' perception of their importance. Take a look at the chart below. If you can complete it quickly, congratulations—you know your customers well. If not, consider consulting your customers. Ask them how they rank your features in order of importance. Their views are helpful for you not only in choosing the right show, but, as you will see later in this book, in giving you valuable insights into the correct signage, product placement, etc., that you should use. If, for example, you find your customers' primary need is price, then offering a "show special" at your booth might be helpful. If you find that status ranks high on your customers' wish list, then participating in a show that attracts the cream of the crop will make a lot of sense.

Take the time to compete the table below.

WHAT'S MOST IMPORTANT TO YOUR CUSTOMER?				
	High	*Medium*	*Low*	*Not at All*
Price				
Brand name				
Status				
Variety				
Convenience				
Warranty				
Salespeople				
Customer service				
Promotion				
Payment terms				
Quality				
Flexibility				
Other				

By understanding demographic, psychographic, and behavioral data as well as causation, you have developed a clear portrait of your customers or perhaps your analysis may reveal more than one customer profile. Creating individual customer profiles is a crucial step in focusing your marketing effort and ensuring that you are indeed in the right show. Having developed these vignettes, your next question is, "How can I reach them?" That's what this chapter is about. You need to be sure that the show you select will reach the right audience at the right time.

RANK YOUR CUSTOMER PROFILES IN ORDER OF PRIORITY

Ask yourself which targeted group will deliver the greatest return on your investment. Let's say you have identified three distinct users of your product or service. Your ROI question will let you know where to expect the biggest bang for your buck. Now, when faced with various potential show selections, you can simply examine the audience quality, see where it fits in your priority, and decide.

Let's assume the following:

- Customer profile 1 is your "A" priority.
- Customer profile 2 is your "B" priority.
- Customer profile 3 is your "C" priority.

Your analysis may look like this:

CUSTOMER PROFILE RANKING			
Show	*Total Audience*	*Percentage Who Fit Criteria*	*Potential Audience*
New York	12,000	Customer 1, 3%	360
		Customer 2, 2%	240
Chicago	8,000	Customer 1, 4%	320
		Customer 2, 0%	
Atlanta	10,000	Customer 1, 10%	1,000
		Customer 2, 3.5%	350
Toronto	7,500	Customer 1, 14%	1,050
		Customer 2, 8%	600

In the above example, Toronto is the clear winner, although the total overall traffic is smaller than the other three shows. Toronto provides you with the best audience and that is what exhibiting is really all about.

WHERE DO YOU FIND PLACES TO EXHIBIT?

The first step is to state your objectives and then create a customer profile. Now it's time to choose a place to exhibit.

You have many choices. Exhibit marketing assumes many forms and encompasses more than the traditional trade show (although trade show exhibiting is still the most popular segment of event marketing). Here are seven popular exhibiting opportunities you can choose from. Look at this list and see where you stand the best chance of meeting your "A" and "B" priority customers in the time that each event affords you.

TYPES OF EVENTS: COMPARISONS

Type of Event	Description	Audience Range	Benefits to Customer	Benefits to User	Disadvantages
Trade show exhibit	Participation in an existing trade show	Will attract all those interested in a common theme or industry	A wide range of exhibitors and activities under one roof	Being compared to the competition	Opportunities for attention and attendee time are limited
Truck tour	A traveling event that is housed in a truck, van, or other motorized vehicle	Very specific since the display travels to their location	Can ask relevant questions at a relaxed pace; no travel time required	Control over audience quality	Very expensive; a great deal of preparation must be done to ensure audience quality
Road shows	A traveling event held in local rented facilities	Reach regional audiences	Attendance is often by appointment	Control over audience quality; can customize message for each audience	Can range from low to high budget, which also includes having personnel on the road
Seminars	An educational program focused on customers and prospects	Can focus on one element such as technical or administrative personnel	Can learn and network	Can learn and network	Run the risk of attendance being influenced by things beyond your control, i.e., weather, traffic, etc.

continued

Type of Event	Description	Audience Range	Benefits to Customer	Benefits to User	Disadvantages
Hospitality events	An event that can be held on its own or in conjunction with other events; usually a social setting where customer relationships are enhanced	Has broad appeal, but can be tailored to suit a specific audience need	Great for networking among colleagues and industry personnel	Great for PR and networking	Tough to sell in a social situation; clients are often skeptical; the services of an independent event planner are often necessary
Stand-alone	These are opportunities in malls, lobbies, boardrooms, reception areas, etc.	Appeals to a very general audience base	A surprise addition to a normal shopping experience	An inexpensive way of getting value from a display that is not otherwise being used	Not well targeted; a shotgun approach
Professional conferences	An educationally oriented event focusing on one professional group	Very targeted delegates who are all part of one professional group	Great place to network, learn, and see relevant products and services	Tight control over audience quality	Exhibit traffic can be sporadic
Private shows	A trade show organized exclusively for one vendor or buying group	Can be very targeted as audience members are usually by invitation only	Very focused shopping experience	Blocks out the competition	Large organizational responsibility that might be subcontracted if your event is large enough

HOW TO CHOOSE THE RIGHT EVENT

Choosing the right event for you is a matter of style, taste, logistics, budget, ability, and geography. Geography is an important factor since it refers to your marketing reach and begs the question "Where is the best place to reach my targeted customer?" Think of your geographic reach as three tiers: regional, national, and international.

Tier 1: Regional Events

How large a regional audience you attract varies according to the type of event you choose. If you select a trade show, you might be able to influence visitors from as far away as 200 miles (320 kilometers) from the site. A mall exhibit, however, will likely attract only people from the immediate neighborhood. Similarly, a seminar is usually held in a local venue with invited guests drawn from the surrounding area. However, a truck tour will enable you to focus on one tightly defined area at a time. Regional initiatives are also excellent venues for a business-to-consumer market.

Tier 2: National Events

National events attract participants from across the country. They are usually wider in scope and focus. The geographic reach also affects the type of attendee. For example, a local show or event might attract technical folks, while an international show might attract senior executives. It may include a national product launch involving nationwide advertising and promotions so the event will be offered in a number of major cities. This will encourage customers to attend the show in the closest or most convenient city to them.

National trade shows usually occur at the same time each year and attract exhibitors and attendees from a wide geographic area. These events are usually business-to-business marketing events.

Tier 3: International Events

In the international arena there are fewer events, but they are designed to attract visitors from a wider geographic area. These events are usually well established and well known in the industry, and because they are often timed according to business cycles, they become a must-see event for attendees. They attract all levels of decision makers. While these events draw attendees from around the globe, they also have a local appeal.

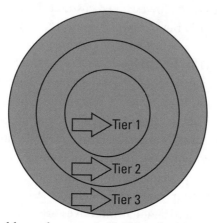

Exhibitors should not be surprised if local visitors are interested in seeing products and services that will be at their retailers in the months to come. So, while the focus is on business-to-business marketing, there is also an opportunity to create some business-to-consumer awareness.

In the figure above, you first choose your target group in order of priority, then follow the appropriate arrow in the direction of the types of events that they are most likely to attend.

MATCH YOUR EVENT WITH YOUR REACH	
Type of Event	*Market Reach*
Trade show exhibit	Tier 1, 2, and 3
Truck tours	Tier 1 and 2
Road shows	Tier 1 and 2
Seminars	Tier 1
Hospitality events	Tier 1, 2, and 3
Professional conferences	Tier 1, 2, and 3
Stand-alone	Tier 1
Private shows	Tier 1 and 2

WHERE TO FIND SUITABLE EVENTS

On-line Directories

In the past, hard-copy annual directories resembling big-city telephone books were filled with useful trade show information. Now most of them can be found on-line. A web search of trade show directories will result in many choices such as *www.Expoworld.net* or *www.TSNN.com*. Choose the industry, location, and dates, and you will find many choices. Each show listing provides a thumbnail sketch of individual shows with exhibitor numbers, exhibition floor size, numbers of attendees, venue address, event description, and exhibitor and visitor contact information. With this basic tool you can contact the individual show organizers to determine if the show is the right one for you.

Various government agencies have useful web sites. They are industry based and can open the door to many potential exhibiting opportunities.

Show management companies such as *www.dmgworldmedia.com* and *www.reedexpo.com* have sites related to their own shows. In addition to specific show information, they also provide a host of other relevant tips, such as hotel registration, travel assistance, show registration, space booking, and so on. On-line directories have become a valuable source of information for any exhibitor in search of a show.

Suppliers

Suppliers usually have their ears to the ground and have insider knowledge of specific industries. Your good relationship with your suppliers allows you to tap into this wealth of information. Your suppliers may also be working with organizations that serve similar markets and may know about outstanding events. They also have a tremendous built-in network with national and international representatives. See if your rep can get in touch with others who might be able to provide you with event intelligence.

Customers

Customer feedback may include opinions on many of the events they attend as well as the reasons why they go. Ascertaining what they do at these events can help you plan your event more effectively. If you listen carefully, your customers can be a great source of ideas.

Associations

The Center for Exhibition Industry Research reports that three-quarters of all the shows in North America are owned by not-for-profit associations. For such associations, show sponsorship is a crucial service to their members. Check your industry association web site or talk to your association representative about upcoming show opportunities.

Trade Magazines

Whether trade magazines are owned by an association or an independent publisher, their mandate is to serve their industry. In addition to publisher a calendar of upcoming shows and events, they also cover many of the events. Adding magazine writers to your network is a good idea because through them you can glean first-hand information about shows and events that you are considering. Your relationship with the media can also open the door to many new opportunities.

Keep Your Eyes and Ears Open

The trick to finding new opportunities is to remove your blinkers and see an entire world of ideas and opportunities in unexpected places: an offhand comment at an industry dinner; a conversation overheard at the squash club; or a chat with other exhibitors on the show floor. While I have listed a few sources in this chapter, the truth is that the number is limited only by your imagination. All you have to do is to keep your eyes and ears open.

IN CONCLUSION

Finding the right show is difficult. Don't jump at the first opportunity that knocks on your door. You have lots of choices. Take your time and do your homework. The right show is a blend of audience, cost, and logistics. Good event selection is a solid base upon which the rest of your exhibit program is built.

Managing the Physical Aspects

"Before a painter puts a brush to his canvas
he sees his picture mentally....
Is the picture one you think worth painting?"
— Thomas Dreier —

Create Your Three-Dimensional Marketing Experience

"We had the experience but missed the meaning."
— T.S. Eliot —

CREATING THE EXPERIENCE

Before we examine the nuts and bolts of creating the physical display, let's step back and look at what you are trying to accomplish. All too often, the emphasis is on appearance rather than creating an effective structure that advances your organization toward accomplishing its real goals. Don't fall victim to Oscar Wilde's quip, "It is only shallow people who do not judge by appearance." Exhibit builders have told me that when asking clients about their objectives, they might reply, "Our objective is to integrate an existing piece of hardware into our new display," or "We want to include a hospitality area." These are not objectives. These are ideas to save money or to add a new element to the display. Objectives are different and require forethought. (For a review of the objective-setting process, go back and reread Chapter 1.)

Once you are clear about why you are exhibiting, look at the big picture. Think about the experience you want to give your visitors and keep these following three elements in mind: interest, memorability, and connectivity. The dictionary definition of "experience" is "something that happens to somebody." What happens to your visitors in your booth is not something they had planned for themselves but is an experience that you have carefully orchestrated for them.

INTEREST

The most common question exhibitors ask themselves is, "How can I stand out in the crowd and differentiate myself from the competition?" At a show, your real competition is other exhibitors who are vying for attention from the same visitors you want to approach. Being oblivious of their efforts may put your exhibit plans in jeopardy of being "out-boothed" by a neighbor. Exhibitors will scramble to include a grab bag of attention-getting ideas, including: prizes, draws, eye-catching graphics, and demonstrations. All these have merit, yet there must be a solid strategic rationale for every activity that occurs in your booth. It boils down to what works and what doesn't. The answer lies in understanding show visitors and what arouses their interest in one booth rather than another.

It's not easy for show visitors—there is so much to see, so many exhibitors, so much information, and so little time to take it all in. Walking through a show is like drinking from a fire hose—it is simply too much. The result is overload—the visitors' attention span dwindles, making them incapable of absorbing new information. They are overstimulated and don't know where to focus first.

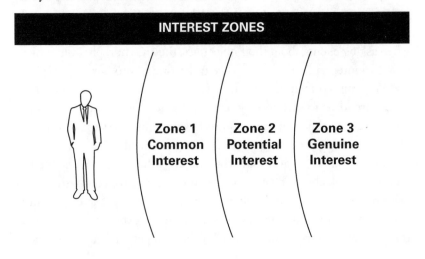

INTEREST ZONES

| | Zone 1 Common Interest | Zone 2 Potential Interest | Zone 3 Genuine Interest |

Some visitors already have a good idea of who you are and want to visit your booth. It could be the result of your aggressive pre-show promotion campaign, your company's reputation, word of mouth, or because of a memorable experience they had at your last show booth. Such visitors will come to your exhibit because they had planned to and nothing will stop them. Another group attends the show with no plans to stop by your booth. They have satisfied their show needs and are now looking to discover other show opportunities—new suppliers, interesting products, etc. This walk-by traffic comes across your exhibit by chance. Ignoring the potential for new business from such visitors would be foolish. Although visitors have diverse reasons for coming to a show, they tend to ignore things that don't grab their attention quickly.

Attracting a visitor's interest is a methodical process. Each visitor needs to pass through three distinct zones of interest. It all happens very quickly—people start at zone 1, then move quickly to zone 3. All visitors will respond to zone 1, but the closer you can bring them to zone 3, the greater the probability you have of conducting business with them. As they move through each zone, you are tempting your visitor to move further into the booth, first visually and then in person.

Before you plan your booth layout and your attention-getting techniques, take a moment to think of your booth in terms of its "interest zones." When you ignore the attention-getting aspect of your display, you risk everything. Miguel de Cervantes said, "Take away the cause and the effect ceases."

Zone 1: Common Interest

Visitors walking down the aisle are like kids in a candy store. In the candy store they see everything and nothing—all at once. They are blown away by the "cool" displays and mountains of candy. Their focus is on one thing only—instant gratification. While trade show visitors are focused on their shopping needs, they are also overburdened with information. The result—visitors do not absorb 90 percent of the words in any trade show. Their instant gratification is more than the bag of Smarties. It might be a warm fuzzy feeling that

comes with recognizing images in the exhibitor's booth, or the wit
and humor in the display, or an instant understanding that a solution
to a buying problem is at hand . In zone 1, attention-getting, show
stopping graphics play an important role. As visitors walk by, they are
immediately attracted to a universal message represented in dynamic
graphics. Smaller pictures won't do the trick.

Other techniques that attract visitors at zone 1 include the presence of recognizable personalities, in-booth games, moving lights,
sampling, and draws for prizes with a universal appeal.

Zone 2: Potential Interest

After piquing visitors' interest, you need to methodically draw them
further into your booth. Your display needs to make a connection.
Make sure your corporate marketing messages, colors, and images are
reinforced in the booth. Getting your visitors' mental bells to ring
can come from something as simple as a marketing "tag line." They
are short statements (less than seven words) that tell your visitors how
your products and services provide a solution for them. Do you recognize any of these? "Don't leave home without it." "Drivers
wanted." "Zoom zoom." "Just do it." Or "The world on time." Get
the message?

Your booth is an opportunity to reinforce your marketing messages from radio, television, print, posters, billboards, or wherever
else you market.

In this zone your signs can go into a bit of detail, but not too
much. Perhaps some of the major benefits of the product can be
posted, but no more. At zone 2 you might also use a draw, catalogs,
product demonstrations, and videos.

Zone 3: Genuine Interest

Here you spark visitors' desire to learn more by encouraging them to
venture further into the booth. Here your signs can give even more
information. In-booth signs strategically placed in zone 3 are
designed to help boothers in their presentation. One-on-one presentations and in-booth seminars take place in zone 3.

INTEREST ZONES: A SUMMARY		
Zone	*Motivation*	*Visitor's Interest*
1. Common interest	• Attention to a universal message. • Can include an element of fun, but most of all a clear, unforgettable message that links the exhibitor with a universal need.	• Will stop and take note. • Is willing to be drawn further into the exhibit for more information. • Curiosity piqued. • Avoids eye contact.
2. Potential interest	• Makes a connection. • Sees the potentials of a solution to a shopping need. • Will spend more time, although not sure whether or not the solution fits.	• Is less likely to continue walking by. • Will begin to focus on detail. • Develops a curiosity that demands answers. • Attempts to make eye contact with the exhibitor for the first time.
3. Genuine interest	• Recognizes positive connections between need and solution. • Develops a genuine interest in acquiring more information on how the exhibit can satisfy their shopping needs.	• Will watch demonstrations. • Talks to the boother. • Examines product more closely. • Asks questions and takes notes.

Understanding interest zones helps you create a logical sequencing of signs and fixtures as well as all the other peripheral tools used to attract attention. It is the underlying force that differentiates a display that works from those that do not.

MEMORABILITY

Wouldn't it be great if all of us had photographic memories so we could recall, in vivid detail, everything we ever saw? If this were true, it would make the job of marketers much simpler. However, psychologists tell us that less than 1 percent of Western adults possess this power of eidetic or vivid imagery. If you ask the average adult about his or her memory, the person is likely to confess to having memory shortfalls.

Memory is more than recalling birthdays, anniversaries, phone numbers, and names. It is the ability to recall information needed to solve problems. Remembering is defined as "to retain in the memory, keep in mind ... to think of again." Forgetting is defined as "to cease or fail to remember."

University of Toronto professor Endel Tulving's work on memory has resulted in many interesting conclusions. One he calls "state-dependent memory," which he explains as the "effective retrieval clues are those which help to re-create the original event or experience." In marketing terms, this assumes two things: the original experience was noteworthy and there were other clues that reinforced the memory of the original experience. The bottom line is that an overall experience has a better chance of being remembered than its individual details. For example, you recall the Yankees won the game, but can't remember the score.

The exhibit manager's job is to create a holistic experience from beginning to end that is so strong and meaningful that the visitor will be less likely to forget it. Your goal is to plan an exhibit that will minimize those things that people tend to forget and emphasize those things they will remember. What will they remember? It might be one of the following:

- The overall professionalism of your booth
- A special feature such as a waterfall,
- The welcoming feeling of attentive booth staff
- The cohesiveness of an overall theme
- Sound, lights, hospitality, entertainment etc.

CONNECTIVITY

Connectivity is what visitors experience in zone 2. When a connection is made, bells go off and visitors say, "Hey, something is familiar here!" They recognize something in your display that reminds them of something they saw in an ad, on a store shelf, or at a previous exhibition. Connectivity is a result of branding—the creation of something familiar that customers begin to recognize as part of your company or product. It is the sum total of all the promises and perceptions you have created. A brand works corporately only when it is supported by every level of the organization. When you go to a McDonald's restaurant anywhere in the world, you expect a similar memorable experience—that's branding.

Marketers sometimes have to wrestle with regionalizing the brand. The McDonald's experience is pretty much the same whether you are eating Big Macs or McSushi. The image of Colonel Sanders is still Colonel Sanders even when his look is Asian, and Coca-Cola bottles are the same worldwide even if the ingredients have been adjusted to meet the locally perferred sweetness level. In other words, the image remains the same. All this tells exhibit managers that while the experience should be strong enough to recognize, every event attracts a different audience and some regionalization may be necessary. You may need to adjust certain elements of your plans to satisfy local cultural tastes and preferences. These can include signage, graphics, colors, product mix, and brochures, etc., while maintaining the common look and feel of the brand.

Interest, memorability, and connectivity are not mutually exclusive. Rather, they are three elements that must be carefully balanced and integrated.

DEVELOPING YOUR DISPLAY NEEDS ANALYSIS

Before you visit your display company to purchase a booth, you need to do some homework. Imagine walking into a clothing store where a frisky salesperson introduces himself and then proceeds to show you everything. What would your reaction be? You would probably want to get out of there as fast as possible. Buying a booth is considerably more complicated than matching a shirt and tie. If you pick the wrong shirt, you can replace it. If styles change, no problem, you can change along with the trends. But a booth can last five or six years or longer in some cases, so even before you walk into the display builder's showroom, you should complete your needs analysis.

By doing your homework in advance, you will save time and be clear about what you need. Now, when the display builder's salesperson approaches, you simply hand the salesperson the file and say, "Let's go through the steps together." That's efficiency. Here are the steps.

1. *Reasons for Exhibiting*
    Excuse the repetition, but I hope you get the point—everything revolves around your objectives. Clearly articulating your objectives is crucial. However, here is additional information your booth builder needs to know.

2. *Your Corporate History*
    Include background information about your organization—who you are, what you do, and how you do it.

3. *Your Competition*
    You should also describe your competitors. Don't assume that the booth builder knows everyone. In fact, the booth builder may also be working for the competition. Gather as much strategic intelligence as possible to describe your competitor's presence at shows. Take a good look at your competitors, and note the size and location of their exhibits. Try to find out which shows and events they attend. Describe the style of their exhibits. Are they open or closed? Do they employ lots of special effects? Do they have in-booth activities? What colors do they use? Do they use a custom or system display?

4. *Your Budget*
    Companies are often reluctant to discuss the budget. Perhaps it comes down to a simple mistrust of the person you are dealing with

or it could stem from your inexperience in not knowing where to start. In any event, it is important to have some budget in mind.

In Chapter 2 you learned the skills of managing the fiscal components of exhibit marketing. Part of that responsibility is having an idea of what things cost. Reach out to your network and talk to your industry colleagues. Find out what they have done, who did it for them, and what it costs. Associations like the Trade Show Exhibitors Association (TSEA) offer you a chance to increase the scope of your network. When you attend trade shows or other events, walk around and see what other people are doing. Talk to exhibitors about the efficiency of their structures. Trade shows like the Trade Show about Trade Shows (TS2), the Exhibitor Show, the Exhibiting Show in England, or Expo Systems in Brazil are excellent venues to gather intelligence about costs. These activities should give you a ballpark figure for an appropriate budget.

5. *Show Plans*

Developing a good plan takes time. Ideally, you should know a year in advance where you are exhibiting. There are always new opportunities that crop up at the last minute, but most of your plan needs time to develop. Planning should include a carefully constructed list of each venue, the amount of booth space you require, the booth configuration (in-line, end-of-aisle, peninsula, island), and any restrictions such as back walls, height, building structures, columns, etc. You can achieve significant economies of scale by creating one display that can be reconfigured to meet several different exhibit situations.

6. *Who Is Your Target Audience?*

In Chapter 3 you learned the importance of creating a customer profile. This information is as important to you as it is to your booth builder. Will there be access for special needs visitors? What type of materials and look do you need to create an experience that will attract your target audience? Are there cultural considerations to be addressed to attract visitors in the country where you will be exhibiting?

7. *Marketing Materials*

    At this stage, it is important to review all your marketing materials and decide on which images and messages in your display need to be reinforced. Look at your newspaper and magazine ads, corporate brochures, product literature, promotional items, corporate videos, television or radio commercials, and presentation materials. It's a mistake to try to include everything in your exhibit. You need to establish priorities. Deciding which components are nice to have versus those that you must have requires brainstorming with some of your colleagues. The issue here is connectivity. This is your chance to reinforce other marketing messages and help visitors connect more quickly to your booth. If your display builder is doing an effective job, he or she will make suggestions that might eliminate some of your graphics or messages. Listen and be flexible. They are the booth design experts.

8. *Your History*

    In Chapter 2 you learned about conducting a post-show briefing and the importance of keeping an exhibit file, which is a record that logs your exhibiting history—its successes and failures and the types and numbers of events you participate in. Review each item with an open mind. Capitalize on the things that clearly worked in previous exhibits. Don't be guilty of throwing the baby out with the bath water. Identify and eliminate those that didn't work. In addition, keep photographs, drawings, and plans in this exhibit file. These will all be helpful as you begin creating or refurbishing an exhibit.

9. *Product Displays*

    A frustrated booth builder recently told me this story. A customer walked into his showroom, walked over to a particular display, and said, "That's the one I want."

The salesperson said, "Can I ask you a few questions about how you are going to use it?"

"That's the one I want," the customer said emphatically, "so let's not waste each other's time."

"I'm just trying to make sure you are purchasing something that will do the job for you. All these displays are different," the salesperson said.

"Are you going to sell me that display or not?"

So, the salesperson sold him the display.

A couple of weeks later the customer was on the phone, yelling and screaming. "You sold me a piece of junk. I put it up, put my products on the shelves, and the whole thing collapsed."

"What was the product?" the salesperson asked.

"Industrial gears," he said.

"And how much did they weigh?" the salesman asked, knowing immediately what the problem was.

"About 400 pounds," the customer answered.

"If you had told me that when I asked you what your booth needs were, I would have told you it was the wrong display."

Such stories happen all the time. Think about what you are going to display and some of the options. Are your products better on a counter or mounted on a wall? Do you have demonstration materials such as large screens, interactive video stations, Internet access, kiosks, etc.? Will the booth support these?

10. *In-Booth Activities*

Your in-booth activities add to the experience you are creating. These activities can include such things as entertainment, demonstrations, educational events, Internet access, hospitality, games, draws, and sampling.

The activities you choose should complement your overall exhibiting objective. They need to be well thought out and attention given to the logistics of orchestrating them. If you are planning an in-booth event, ensure that the structure you select will accommodate the activity.

11. *The Business Environment*

Your exhibit is a place of business for a very few hectic days. You must take care to ensure that you have created a practical place to conduct business. If you are building a retail display where purchases will be made, you will need transaction tools such as a cash register, shopping bags, and credit card transaction machines. For most exhibits, you will also need to take into account storage, staff's personal effects, safety equipment, a reception area, literature dispenser, and meeting areas.

YOUR NEEDS ANALYSIS SUMMARY	
Your Design Needs Analysis	*Description*
1. Reasons for exhibiting	Focus on objectives.
2. Corporate history	Corporate background information.
3. Competition	Identify your competitors Exhibiting practices.
4. Budget	Develop a realistic budget.
5. Show plans	Create a holistic, integrated show experience.
6. Your target	Develop a customer profile.
7. Marketing materials	Catalog samples of all current marketing materials.
8. History	Chronicle past exhibit experiences.
9. Product display	List products, samples, or other materials to be displayed.
10. In-booth activities	Develop a list of other attention-getting activities.
11. The business environment	List the tools you need to do business.

CREATE A REQUEST FOR PROPOSAL (RFP)

Now that your needs analysis is complete, the next step is to create a request for proposal (RFP). The RFP allows an exhibit builder to quote accurately as it contains all the elements required. It also lets you compare various bids—apples with apples.

If you live in a major city, look up display builders in your local telephone or on-line directory and you will find numerous listings of relevant companies. Sending your RFP to all of them is clearly a waste of everyone's time. Narrowing the list to two or three display builders makes more sense.

Your Short List

Some of the information you need to know includes the builder's exhibit lines, history, products, warranty program, creative capabilities, personalities, customer base, industry knowledge, graphics capabilities, and additional services such as install and dismantle (I & D) and storage. Reading through the columns of names in your local telephone or on-line directory is not the most efficient way of creating a short list. A better approach starts with your own observations at shows and events. As an exhibit manager, it is important to walk through as many shows as possible, and not just those shows catering to your industry, but *all* shows. As a professional show visitor, you look for things the average visitor misses, such as the quality of exhibits. Look for exhibitors who display products or services similar to yours. They don't have to be competitors but companies who face similar exhibiting challenges. If you have a heavy or bulky product, look for exhibitors who are displaying similar items. If you offer a service and are not sure what attracts visitors, look at similar service providers and see what they are doing. The more you observe, the more knowledgeable you become and you will slowly begin to distinguish exhibits that work from those that don't.

Once you have identified the exhibit hardware you want, try to get the name of the person in the other organization that contracted for the booth. Ask him or her to spare you a few minutes either during the show or perhaps by phone after the show to run through some questions. You will want to know how well the supplier understood the company's exhibiting needs. Were they reliable? Did they provide helpful service? And, most important, would they deal with them again?

This is a time-consuming process, but your choice of a booth builder is important. Since you will have to live with the consequences of your decision for years, you need to spend the time at the beginning to get it right the first time. Remember, act in haste; repent at leisure.

Certain names of display builders will likely come up over and over again. When this happens and the comments are positive, you are on the road to finding a potential candidate. Keeping your list short helps you manage the process efficiently. Settle on two or three candidates and send your RFP to each name on the list.

ABC Company
10 Main Street
Everywhere, Canada
LOP 1NO
1-800-358-6079

Request for Proposal
for the design and building of the corporate exhibit
Date: March 26, 2004
RFP Deadline: May 15, 2004
RFP sent to:
  1. Big Booth Manufacturing
  2. Great Idea Exhibits
  3. It's SHOWBIZ Displays

This RFP covers the creation, fabrication, installation, dismantling, and storage of the corporate exhibit booth.

1. Exhibiting objective
2. Corporate background
3. Competition
4. Budget
5. Show plans
6. Target audience
7. Marketing materials

---

8. Exhibit history
9. Product displays
10. In-booth activities
11. The business environment

If you have any questions or need clarification, please contact
_____.

Managing the Selection Process

There are several ways to manage the selection process. You can simply call each of your short-listed companies and ask them if they are
interested in receiving your RFP. Another approach is to hold a
design conference. Invite the candidates to attend a meeting that you
host during which you introduce them to your company, talk about
your products and services, review the RFP, and answer their questions. This is an efficient way of ensuring that everyone is working
from the same page. It is also helpful for the candidates to know
against whom they are competing. In addition, the Q & A session
often uncovers areas you have omitted in your planning.

After the initial design conference, invite each of your short-
listed candidates to a presentation meeting. Each is allocated a time
slot to present his or her company's solutions. This gives you a chance
to review all the proposals at once, putting you and the selection committee in a strong position to make a quick decision.

Before the presentation meetings you should look at each major
section of your RFP and give it a weighted value, say 1 to 10, with 1
being the lowest and 10 the highest score. Each member of your decision committee rates each presentation based on the RFP criteria.
After adding up the scores, you will have an excellent basis for your
ultimate decision.

THE DESIGN SCHEDULE

Once the final decision has been made, it's time to start building your
display. Setting up a schedule is important for monitoring the

progress. Your successful candidate knows your exhibit schedule and the target dates. Obviously a small booth requires less monitoring than a big one. When you establish benchmark dates for progress reviews, you eliminate many of the last-minute surprises. Here is a typical progress schedule.

YOUR NINETY-DAY SCHEDULE
Day   1–10: Create the initial design.
Day 11–30: Present design revisions.
Day 31–73: Construct the booth.
Day 74–81: Set up and make last-minute revisions to the booth.
Day 82–90: Ship the booth to the show and assemble.

IN CONCLUSION

You now understand what your exhibit is supposed to accomplish and you have created your RFP. Now it's time to get down to the details that answer the question: "How?"

Your Display—the Nuts and Bolts

"One leak will sink the ship."
— John Bunyan —

Your display builder is the professional. He or she has spent years studying all the design elements and has a tremendous depth of experience to guide you. Knowing the questions you should ask at your first meeting will make you a better purchaser. Here is an overview of what you can expect from a builder and what you should question.

SYSTEM: CUSTOM OR HYBRID?

Your choice of booth hardware used to be a simple decision between two distinct categories—system or custom. Recently booth technology has changed dramatically, blurring the line between the two. A system booth was one that could be put together in seconds since it was manufactured like a giant Meccano set with interlocking parts that unfolded from shipping crates. Custom booths, however, are built from scratch for the exhibitor.

While in some cases there are displays that are totally customized, often you will see hybrids that combine both system and custom elements.

COLOR

Color is one of the biggest influences on the human psyche. Whether we are aware of it or not, color plays an important part in our daily lives. Alice Walker, in her book *The Color Purple*, wrote: "I think it pisses God off if you walk by the color purple in a field somewhere and don't notice it." Color affects all of our senses and can have a direct effect on our mood. Choose the wrong colors and you can turn people away from an otherwise effective display. But if you choose well, color can add considerable value to visitors' overall experience of your booth.

Color theory originates from the color wheel, first developed in 1666 by Sir Isaac Newton. This is a circular diagram showing a logical arrangement of color hue.

The color wheel starts with the primary colors of red, yellow, and blue. These three primary colors are combined into secondary colors, which are green, orange, and purple. The tertiary colors are formed by mixing the secondary colors, creating yellow-orange, red-orange, red-purple, blue-purple, blue-green, and yellow-green. The color wheel is the logical sequencing of these tertiary colors.

Once you understand the color wheel, you can create color harmony. Harmony is something that is visually attractive. It engages visitors and creates a sense of balance in the visitors' visual experience. When things are not harmonious, they are perceived as boring or chaotic. Harmony is created by mixing and matching colors on the color wheel. The three basic formulas for harmony are analogous, complementary, and nature.

Analogous colors are side by side on the color wheel. Complementary colors, however, are those that are directly opposite each other on the color wheel and create maximum contrast without offending the visitor. The third element is based on colors in nature, which provide perfect color harmony such as a combination of red, yellow, and green. If you are creating an exhibit program that will be used internationally, then using colors in nature will eliminate many problems since people throughout the world make similar color associations regardless of culture.

The rule of thumb is that harmony links things together and contrasting colors separate them.

Psychologists have created generalizations about colors and what they mean. While this list is generic, it is a good beginning point for your discussion with your display builder. Your decision on color starts with an understanding of the exhibit experience you are trying to create.

THE MEANING OF COLORS	
Color	*Meaning*
Blue	Reputable, loyal, cool. This is the color of truth, serenity, and harmony. It helps soothe the mind. Blue can generate a sense of well-being.
Green	Links with nature; is solid. This is the color of harmony and balance. It is a restful color that promotes hope, stability, and peace.
Red	Dangerous, strong, aggressive, dynamic. It is the color of energy, excitement, and vitality.
Black	Elegance, power, individuality. This is a deep, sophisticated, and dramatic color. It can also be powerful, aloof, and intimidating.
Yellow	Bright, optimistic, envious, greedy. It is a warm color that is also the color of intellect. It can be used for mental stimulation. Its cheeriness can stimulate activity.
Orange	Stimulating, energetic. It is a warm color that represents ripeness, warmth, and happiness. It can promote a feeling of happiness.
Brown	Solid; links with nature (earth), conservative.
Purple	This is the color that connects to the spiritual self. It is also associated with noble traits, love, truth, and justice.
White	Brightness, clarity, purity, cleanliness. White is the color of purity. It symbolizes light, innocence, and joy. It can give an atmosphere of coolness.
Gray	Neutral, modest, unobtrusive. Silver is the color of peace, and gray is like white in its purity. Together they represent a rich, strong image.
Gold	Majesty, glory, pride.
Pastels	Soft, sweet, gentle, romantic. These are colors of equilibrium, especially pastels such as pink, mauve, and lavender. They can be soothing colors.

Source: © 1999 Shopfittings on line.com.au.

Which Color Should Dominate—the Color of the Product or the Display?

Color ties your display to your product. When it is well done, color creates a visual image that sparks the imagination of the visitor. Your ultimate goal is to focus attention on your product with the display as background. While this is the general rule, some products in themselves are rather uninspiring visually and need the help that the display can offer. If your products fall into this category—for example, products such as small automotive parts, some hardware items, software, certain packaged goods, etc.—then you must create a display that compensates visually for what your product lacks. For these examples, a strong color for the display will draw attention to the product, yet not overshadow it. You can select contrasting colors on the color wheel.

If, however, your product easily lends itself to color—such as giftware, linens, clothing, etc.—then highlight the color in the product and let the display blend into the background with subtle tones.

Another scenario is where the product color and display color work in harmony. For example, an upscale line of clothing might be well displayed in an exhibit that has colors that reflect the quality of the product.

Finding the proper blend of product and display color comes down to creativity. To keep on track, follow these guidelines.

Corporate Colors

Color can also play a huge role in achieving connectivity. If you have strong, identifiable corporate colors, use them in your display. You instantly recognize a Coca-Cola booth by the Coca-Cola red. People don't refer to IBM as "Big Blue" for nothing. Again, the color wheel can help you create harmony. Start with your corporate color and find matching colors that will create the appropriate look in your display.

Color and Culture

Various cultures have their unique interpretation of colors. For example, in Japan the color yellow represents grace; in the United States it represents caution. In China the imperial color is yellow. In France red represents aristocracy, while in Britain it is purple. If you are creating a display for a particular culture, it's important to pay attention to its color sensitivities. However, if you are creating a display for a global, multicultural audience, then consider using an array of colors found in nature.

The following chart is adapted from William Horton's, *The Icon Book*. It outlines how color perception changes with different cultures.

CULTURAL PERCEPTIONS OF COLOR				
Color	*Western Europe*	*Japan*	*China*	*Arab Countries*
Red	Danger, aristocracy (France)	Anger, danger	Joy, festive occasions	
Yellow	Caution, cowardice	Grace, nobility, childish, gaiety	Honor, royalty	Happiness, prosperity
Green	Safe, sour, criminality (France)	Future, youth, energy		Fertility, strength
Blue	Masculinity, sweet, calm, authority	Villainy		Virtue, faith, truth
White	Purity, virtue	Death, mourning	Death, mourning	
Black	Death, devil			

One advantage in dealing with exhibit builders who have overseas affiliates is getting the right color information. This section should at least provide you with enough information to ask the right questions about color.

LIGHTING

Today lighting has gone beyond the need to illuminate for survival; it helps us differentiate things and attracts attention.

The human visual system consists of two elements: the eye and the brain. The eye sees and the brain interprets. Well thought-out lighting can focus the visitor's attention on eye-catching graphics and signs, it can enhance the colors of the display, it can create motion, and it can provide an environment conducive to doing business. Since lighting is an essential part of your exhibit plans, you must give it serious attention.

The first step is to understand your lighting choices. There are a variety of lamps and fixtures you can use in displays. Each has its pros and cons.

Incandescent lamps are the typical low-cost, screw-in bulb you use in your home. They provide a yellow light and are most commonly used in clip-on or arm-light fixtures.

Fluorescent lamps are the long tubes of mercury vapor that produce light. They come in a variety of sizes and strengths and are often used to backlight a display. Fluorescents are not flattering to makeup and complexion.

Compact lights are another version of the fluorescent lamp. They are tubes of a smaller diameter and are bent so that two ends fit into a ceramic base. They can be used for a wide variety of color applications and can have a longer life span than the incandescent lamp.

Halogen lights are a type of incandescent bulb that come in various shapes and sizes. The sealed tube contains halogen gas, which produces a bright, white light with low heat. Another version of the incandescent is the Xenon lamp, which has a long life span and produces a high-intensity white light. It creates less heat than halogen bulbs.

A variety of fixtures are available for your display. Here are some criteria for choosing the one to meet your needs.

Versatility

No two exhibit halls are alike. In fact, no two locations in the same exhibit hall are alike. The effect of the facility's ambient lighting will have a considerable impact on your exhibit. You might find yourself directly below powerful, color-altering lights or in a dark area of the exhibit hall. Therefore, you need some versatility in your lighting so you can make last-minute adjustments. Versatility can be as simple as having extra fixtures available or having fixtures that swivel or that can handle different size bulbs.

Color

You have spent a great deal of time and energy to coordinate the colors of your product, signage, and exhibit. Since the impact of those color choices depends on lighting, ensure that the lamps you use are readily available or that you have a stock of replacement lamps in your display kit. Last-minute substitutions can have a negative impact on color.

Style and Design

Think about the last time you purchased lighting fixtures for your home. When you entered the local lighting retailer's showroom, you were immediately overwhelmed by the number of choices. The same holds true for exhibit lighting. The number of options you have seem endless. You can choose from long arms or short arms, rear mounted or free standing, overhead or wall mounted, as long as they fit into your overall concept. The fixtures' function is of primary importance and if they are doing their job properly, chances are that people will notice not the fixtures but the effect they have on your exhibit.

Illuminated Signage

By illuminating specific areas of your exhibit, you create a powerful visual draw. This can be done with fiber optics, LED programmable signs, or fluorescent bulbs backlighting a sign.

Safety

Read the show rules carefully. Ensure that your electrical fixtures do not contravene local fire or safety rules. If in doubt, ask your show organizer. In North America products that are UL-ETL approved are generally the best since most local communities recognize these standards.

Installation

Whether your exhibit manufacturer installs your electrical components, you do it yourself, or have an electrical contractor install it for you, the electrical components of your exhibit should be easy to install, dismantle, and maintain at the show.

FLOORING

Booth flooring is an often-neglected component. Most exhibitors will have some sort of flooring, but the color, quality, and installation are often left to the discretion of the show supplier. Flooring defines the perimeters of your exhibit. It is a visual indicator that the visitor has left the aisle and entered your booth. Flooring can be the perfect accompaniment to your exhibit structure. However, if left to chance, it can act as a barrier. Your flooring considerations should include the look and feel, color, durability, installation, maintenance, and storage.

Look and Feel

Your flooring completes the booth experience. The next time you walk through a show, look at the floor rather than just focusing on the signs and graphics. What do you see? Yes, there are different materials such as wood, carpet, tile, concrete, etc., but look beyond the material to the message. How do you feel walking on this floor? Does this floor complement an experience? What is your impression of this exhibitor? Do you want to spend more time at a particular booth or leave immediately? More often than not, your visitors are walking into your area from the harsh flooring elsewhere in the building. Aisles are typically concrete covered with a thin layer of carpet. You don't have to use thick, plush carpet to distinguish your booth space from the aisle. Rather, your flooring should offer your visitors a respite from the environment they have just left.

Durability

How often do you change the floor covering in your home? If it's carpet and, depending on the number of children you have running around, perhaps every five to ten years. If it's wood, maybe never, so wood is the most durable and should be your number one choice, right? Not necessarily. There is more to durability than longevity. Durability also means ensuring that your floor covering looks brand new each time you set up your display. So, when choosing flooring, consider how many times your booth will be used during the next year or two. How much shipping and handling will be involved? How difficult is it to maintain? Will the flooring you choose stand up to the tortures of moving, installation, storage, and traffic from thousands of visitors? These are more important questions than the overall life span.

Installation

Whether you install the flooring yourself, contract with show labor, or have an outside service provider do it, the flooring must be properly installed. Faulty installations can result in a less-than-professional look, an uncomfortable booth, and be a potential danger to visitors and boothers. Since flooring is the first thing to be installed and the last to be put away, it is the part of your booth hardware that receives the greatest wear and tear. With a carpet you must be careful that it is properly taped on all sides. Consider using an under-pad as well. If you are using wood or tile, all pieces must be joined properly. They should also have a protective coating to prevent damage when heavy hardware and products roll across the surface during setup. Many do-it-yourself exhibitors opt for interlocking flooring. It comes in either wood or carpet interlocking squares, which eliminates the possibility of mistakes. In addition, once the squares have been taken up, they can be stacked in boxes for easy shipping and storage.

Maintenance

Some of the finished hardwood floors have a lifetime guarantee against scuff marks, scratches, and breakage. However, this doesn't prevent them from getting dirty. The same holds true with stain-resistant carpet. Your flooring should be cleaned after every show. Whether it's polished, shampooed, or just vacuumed, regular cleaning will eliminate the buildup of damaging substances. If you leave it until it is installed at the next show and then find a problem, there is a chance that you will not find someone to fix it in time. Such last-minute repairs are also more costly.

Storage

Storing interlocking flooring and hardwood in crates is easy, but storing a rolled-up carpet can be a challenge. Save the heavy plastic wrapping it originally came in for future storage. Ensure that it is well sealed and stored in a clean area of your warehouse. Take note of the temperature and humidity in the storage area. It doesn't take long for mildew to grow. Often exhibitors store entire displays between shows with professionals who keep it in a climate-controlled environment to minimize the risk of damage.

SIGNS AND GRAPHICS

Try this experiment. Sit in a busy mall and look at the signs. What do you see? Starbucks Coffee, Hallmark Cards, Walgreen Drugs, Japan Camera, and so on. What compels you to go to one of these stores—habit, need, or an attractive window display?

Now do the same experiment at a trade show. What do you see? A typical trade show has row after row of exhibitors, all trying to differentiate themselves from their neighbors. Some are more elaborate than the next, while others are simply boring and uninteresting. What prompts you to stop at one exhibitor and not the next? Your motivation to stop is similar to the shopping mall scenario. Perhaps you need the product or service, or you had prior knowledge of the company and had intentionally searched them out, or you were attracted to an exhibitor because of an eye-catching sign or graphic.

At a trade show, habit and need are important factors in attracting visitors. But, like our mall visit, signs and graphics may be what compels a visitor to stop and look. However, a trade show is different because there are competitors within earshot of each other in a relatively small confined space. In a mall, merchants have the advantage of continuous walk-by traffic who might miss you one day, only to drop by the next. Show exhibitors usually get only one kick at the can.

Creating the right signs and graphics is crucial. If you haven't caught visitors' attention within the first four seconds, you have missed them altogether. The right balance of signs and graphics will ensure that the message you are trying to establish is clear, concise, and appealing.

Signs (words) and graphics (pictures) can be divided into two broad categories: showstoppers and informational.

Showstoppers

We have all walked by booths cluttered with pictures representing every possible angle of the product or service or perhaps dozens of photos of successful projects. The chances of having someone stop and examine all these pictures is minimal. Why? Because show visitors, unlike shoppers in a mall, do not have time to browse. The noise, confusion, and general hustle-bustle of the show all contribute to information overload, and excess information only adds to the confusion. Showstopping graphics are powerful oversized pictures that incite the imagination of visitors as they walk by (interest zone 1) with one simple message. If the message is compelling enough, the visitor will stop.

Images of mascots such as Ronald McDonald holding the hands of happy customers or the Taco Bell chihuahua easily lend themselves to the creation of showstoppers. (What would Disney be without Mickey?) Perhaps showstoppers are taken from the lifestyle images that every automotive company uses to promote their new vehicles. Whether the exhibitor is large with enormous creative budgets or a small company with limited assets, the fundamentals are the same.

The same principle applies to signs. Booths that are inundated with signs add to the confusion. Typical signs refer to a product or service, policies, marketing messages, features and benefits, and so on. A simple sign that tells visitors who you are and why they should stop at your booth is far superior to signs depicting every facet of your business. Consider one sign with your name and a marketing message—a tag line—that does not exceed seven words. These seven words are a statement about a new product or service. You can create powerful tag lines to use in all marketing materials, including your display.

Informational

Informational graphics are smaller pictures that help boothers with their presentation. They consist of two or three pictures that boothers can refer to during presentations to help create memorability in the visitors' minds—after hearing and seeing it, they will remember it longer.

Informational signs are used once boothers have the visitors' attention (interest zone 3). A small sign with a quick list of products, services, or features can enhance a one-on-one presentation. Once again, you increase the memorability of your offerings as visitors follow a list rather than relying only on auditory information.

With a bit of planning, the proper signs and graphics can make the world of difference to your booth.

TECHNOLOGY

Adding technology to your booth can work as long as you don't create "Geek World." You have to strike a balance between creating a technology jungle and a smoothly operating booth.

The key to choosing the right technology, like everything else, is to stay focused on your objectives. Why are you at the show? Technology is a tool that can greatly assist you in achieving your goal. It provides a dynamic means of creating attention, telling a story, and enabling interactivity. However, you need to remain germane. If your choice of technology is relevant to your objectives, then you are on the right track. If you are choosing certain technologies just because they are cool and have no relevance to your purpose, you will be wasting time and money.

Technology's role is to enhance your story and visitors' experience. Technology enhances the audio, visual, and sensory attraction of your booth. The problem with technology is that new products come on the market so quickly that they are soon outdated. I once heard an interesting comparison. Just as every dog year is equal to seven human years, every sixty minutes in technology is the equivalent of six human months. Before you make your final arrangements, spend time with your audio-visual consultant. It's his or her job to keep abreast of the latest technological advancements.

Sound

The challenge with sound at a show is that there is simply too much of it. The ambient sound of the facility, the constant noise of neighboring exhibitors, and the frequent public-address system announcements interfere with your efforts to get your message out to visitors. A good mixture of sound equipment will enhance the visitor's ability to concentrate on your booth and presentation while minimizing outside interferences. Sound equipment elements include: microphones, mixers, equalizers, as well as special-effects machines such as reverberators, amplifiers, processors, players, and recorders, not to mention all the accessories needed to connect this equipment without creating extra distractions that will interfere with your booth traffic or detract from your booth's overall visual appeal. Some shows have restrictions on your use of sound equipment. It's always a good practice to check with the show manager first.

Visual

Previously you learned about the three zones of interest. The visual element is dominant in all three interest zones. In zone 1 the visual component can create the "wow" effect with dazzling lasers, strobes, or even an overall booth illumination. In zone 2, lighting will focus the visitor's attention on certain key areas. In zone 3, it's computer-assisted presentations involving smart boards or cameras that can help you tell your story.

Equipment that will enable you to enhance your story visually includes: cameras, projectors, monitors, computers, spotlights, mercury vapor lights, multi-imaging staging, and special-effects lighting.

Sensory

Technology appeals to your visitors' sense of sight and sound as well as touch. Allow them to experience your display through their senses. It can be as simple as a touch screen or live web access. The aroma of brewing coffee or freshly baked cookies appeals to their sense of smell. The sound of soft music or a waterfall will soothe their frazzled nerves. You can also consider creating dramatic effects with artificial smoke, haze machines, or dry ice machines. Once again check with your show manager first.

Ultraviolet light or black light can make fluorescent fabrics and paints look vibrant. The list is endless. If you are considering using technology, talk to your display professional to be sure that your presentation and the technology you choose are properly integrated.

BOOTH CONFIGURATIONS

There are only four traditional configurations. Before you decide which is best, look at the pros and cons of each. For example, you may need additional booth hardware to accommodate a different shape or extra personnel, or there may be added costs involved. Make sure that you factor these costs into your budget and that the change of booth configuration shape makes sense to your overall exhibit program.

In-line

In-line refers to a booth that is located in a straight line beside other exhibitors. It usually means that your one open side is at the front.

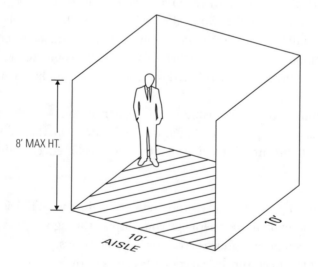

Source: The Canadian Gift & Tableware Association's Publication: "Exhibiting Success"

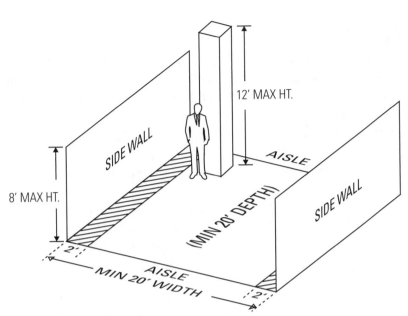

An in-line walk-through

Source: The Canadian Gift & Tableware Association's Publication:
        "Exhibiting Success"

Corner

A corner booth gives you additional exposure to traffic. It is open on
either two or three sides and will give you greater visibility and indi-
viduality than an in-line booth.

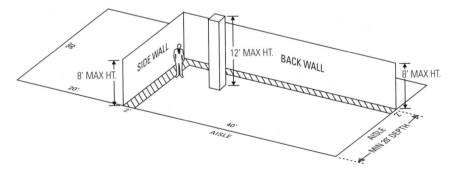

Source: The Canadian Gift & Tableware Association's Publication:
        "Exhibiting Success"

Peninsula

A peninsula is a collection of in-line and corner booths that form a rectangle. One end of the booth is attached to a neighboring exhibitor's booth and it is flanked by three lanes of traffic. It is a great option for exhibitors who are not quite ready to move into an island configuration, but still need extra space.

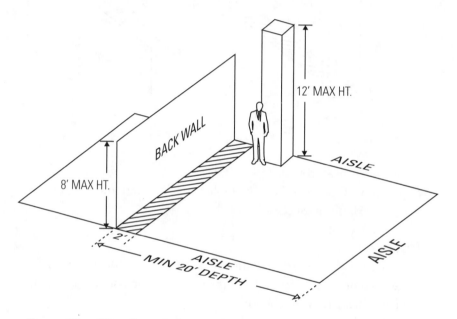

Source: The Canadian Gift & Tableware Association's Publication: "Exhibiting Success"

Island

The island is a self-contained, stand-alone block on the show floor. It provides access from four lanes of traffic around the exhibit area and gives you many more options for creating a dramatic and eye-catching display.

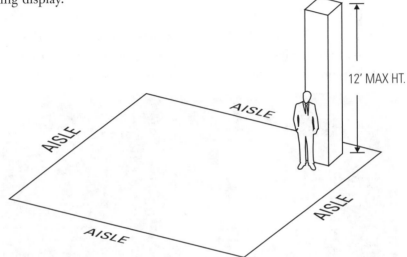

Although you can create sub-shapes, such as an L-shape or a cross-aisle, these are your four basic choices.

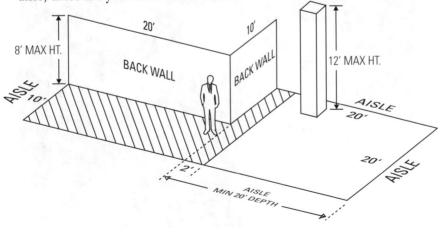

Source: The Canadian Gift & Tableware Association's Publication: "Exhibiting Success"

LAYOUTS

Within the booth configuration you now have to consider the layout of hardware and equipment. There are a multitude of layout schemes to choose from. Here are four traditional examples.

The Classic Diamond

This is the traditional island layout because it leaves the perimeter open to traffic on all sides. It presents a strong visual image. However, there is limited display areas for signs, graphics, and products.

Source: Nimlok Canada Ltd.

The Club

This is a great option for exhibitors who require private areas for client conferences. However, there are a limited number of entrances, which sometimes discourages walk-by traffic.

Source: Nimlok Canada Ltd.

Random

The random display incorporates a number of products and demon-stration areas. It can provide a striking appearance on the show floor and is particularly helpful for exhibitors with more than one focus.

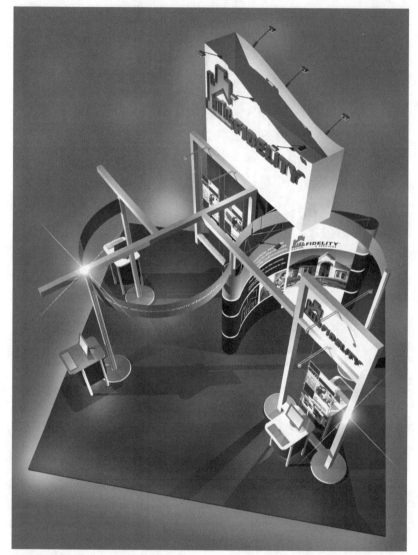

Source: Nimlok Canada Ltd.

Theater

For exhibitors seeking to incorporate in-booth education in the design, theater style is the answer. It provides dedicated seminar space. It is open enough to encourage walk-by traffic, yet can be used in large and small displays.

Source: Nimlok Canada Ltd.

HEIGHT

Eight feet (2.5 meters) is a typical height for most displays and in some shows it is the limit. In others, the height can be two or three storeys high. Some shows allow you to erect large signs or hang ornaments from the ceiling of the facility, while others prohibit this practice. Some shows maintain the 8-foot (2.5-meter) restriction on the back and two sides of an in-line booth, while others restrict the height of the sides to 3 or 4 feet (1 to 1.20 meters). Individual shows and facilities each have height restrictions, so find out what you are allowed to do before planning your display.

Shipping and Drayage

When arranging to get your display to and from the show, engaging a logistics expert can pay off. The overwhelming number of rules and regulations involved in moving your display can drive the most seasoned exhibit manager crazy. And when you exhibit internationally, there is a whole new group of rules to add, not to mention customs and security regulations.

Shipping Containers

The first consideration is what shipping container you will need. Shipping containers are designed and manufactured along with your booth. Their primary purpose is to protect your display against damage so you cannot afford to skimp. Think of your shipping container as a piece of luggage. If the booth is part of a permanent display that will never be moved, you don't need the luggage. However, once you transport your booth, good luggage becomes important.

Protection is the primary consideration and convenience is secondary. If you have a small pop-up display, you will want a container that is easily transportable or will travel in the trunk of your car. Larger and more elaborate booths require better-developed shipping considerations.

There are four broad groups of packing cases to consider.

1. Custom-Designed, Self-Contained Booths

A custom-designed, self-contained booth is a self-pack unit in which the shipping crate is also the booth. When opened, the crate becomes a free-standing booth or part of the booth. This is often used in a road show where the van or trailer is simply backed into the space, opened up, and your booth is on the inside.

2. Custom-Designed Individual Packing Crates

These crates are custom-made for a specific, usually larger booth. They hold the display elements as well as furniture and products. Although they are generally bulkier than other types of containers, for some exhibits they are the only choice. Forklift trucks are usually needed to move these crates, although some have wheels, making them easier to move short distances by hand.

3. Prefabricated Packing Cases

You often see these with many of the system booths on the market. The containers come in a series of standard sizes with inserts to keep your booth and products from shifting during moving. They are often made from moulded plastic and store easily.

4. System Packing Cases

When you purchase a system display, it likely comes with a durable, moulded polyethylene container especially designed to hold your new booth safely. These are generally generic in nature and designed for the specific system. Your customization options have some limitations; however, you can purchase conversion kits to transform these containers into usable countertops, thus solving two problems at once.

The Shipper

The next challenge is choosing a shipping company. There are six main modes of transportation to consider.

Courier Companies

Although courier companies traditionally specialize in delivering small packages, you can use them for short-term shipments, typically overnight or within a day or two. They usually have excellent tracking systems and are a great service for last-minute shipments. However, they may not be prepared to cope with the long line-ups that commonly occur with show deliveries.

Trucking Companies

Traditional trucking companies are usually set up for dock-to-dock service. Although they handle trade show freight, they may charge extra fees if there is a long wait at the facility. There are also premium-priced, dedicated "white-glove" services in which you hire the entire truck and they do everything possible to get your exhibit to the show on time. The official show supplier is often a trucking company. When they are designated as the official supplier, they can guarantee that they will get your freight to its location on time. They often get priority at the show's loading gate.

Airlines

Airlines are another great last-minute alternative. They have excellent air-cargo tracking systems, but often will not want to organize local cartage. They also may have size and security limitations.

Van Lines

Van lines are skilled at handling high-value freight and they can quote for shipments from door to door. Van lines that specialize in show freight are an excellent option for domestic and cross-border shipments.

Ocean Carriers

Although most exhibitors won't use ocean freight, it is probably the least expensive of all the modes of transportation. While ocean freight is scheduled, ships can encounter delays caused by weather conditions, strikes, and political insurrections. Many exhibitors will contract with local display builders overseas and avoid the shipping hassle altogether. However, for larger displays, ocean freight can be a good idea if there is sufficient lead time.

Logistics Specialists/Freight Forwarders

Freight forwarders are equipped to deal with all modes of transportation. Some specialize in trade show freight and can provide door-to-door service and often negotiate good rates. Freight forwarders are set up to handle just about any customs and other requirements for cross-border and international freight. You can use freight forwarders for one-off, one-time service, or to transport displays and products to a number of shows.

Drayage

Drayage is from the old English word *dragan*, which means "to draw heavy loads." A dray horse was used to pull a dray. In trade show terms, drayage refers to the cost of moving your goods into the show facility. Drayage rules differ from facility to facility. At some there is no charge; at others the show management absorbs the cost; while still others allow you to bring your booth in yourself, but require the exhibitor to pay the cost of setting it up.

The rules for drayage are found in your exhibitors' manual. Here are some important cost-cutting tips.

- Try to bundle your shipments. Sending loose boxes could incur extra charges. There is also a greater chance of loss. If you bundle them all together, be sure to shrink-wrap everything on a skid.
- Read your drayage contract carefully. Never assume that the terms and conditions are the same year after year.
- Avoid sending unnecessary freight. You pay by the 100-pound (45-kilogram) weight (CWT), so pack carefully.
- Label your shipment carefully with your booth number in an obvious place.
- Arrange with the drayage handler and your shipping company in advance and remember to take shipping labels for the return trip.

CUSTOMS AND DUTY

Since 9/11, trans-border shipments and overseas shipments have become more complicated. Talk to your freight forwarder or customs broker about compliance and save yourself countless hours of aggravation and delay. For exhibits and display equipment and machinery that cross many borders before returning home, you might consider a Carnet issued by the International Chamber of Commerce. In simple terms, they serve as passports for goods and eliminate the need for paying duties or deposits on show-related items that leave the country soon after the show.

STORAGE

In cost-per-square-foot terms, exhibit booth space is one of the most expensive pieces of real estate. Be careful not to waste precious space on storage. However, you need a place for your coat and briefcase, shipping crates, samples, and perishables, as well as stationery, literature, business cards, and other business essentials. When developing your display, plan for these things ahead of time. You can create space in cupboards, drawers, or behind partitions that does not detract from the attractiveness of your booth. Make sure your staff understands the importance of keeping the office supplies and personal effects in their designated spaces. A place for everything and everything in its place should be your motto. Without constant vigilance, your display will soon look sloppy and unprofessional. Show management may have a designated storage space that can be negotiated for larger items.

EMERGENCY SUPPLIES BOX

Seasoned exhibitors know from experience that a miscellaneous supplies box can be a lifesaver. While there might be some restrictions on what you can use in different venues, this box of odds and ends filled with last-minute things will help make your setup as effortless as possible. Make an inventory list of the contents. Update the list regularly to track items that have been consumed, lost, or are running low. Add an extra row on the inventory list for suggestions of new items to add to the box. Here is a sample inventory list:

MISCELLANEOUS SUPPLIES BOX INVENTORY			
Date:			
Item	*Quantity*	*Used by*	*Replenishment Quantity*
Duct tape	100 feet		
Carpet tape	100 feet		
Hammer	1		
Screwdriver	1		
Masking tape	100 feet		
Glass cleaner	16 ounces		
Paper towels	2 rolls		
Scissors	1		
First-aid supplies	1 kit (separate inventory)		
Garbage bags	10		
Shipping labels	5		
Markers	2		
Paintbrush	2		
Lightbulbs	6		
Other			
Recommendations			

After each show, designate someone to be responsible for checking the list and replenishing missing items. Over time, the size of the box may grow, but its contents will remain a valuable addition to your display plans. Don't leave home without it!

IN CONCLUSION

Creating a display and getting it to the show and back again in one piece can be a nightmare unless you take the time to plan. However, there is more to a successful show than logistics. Lets turn our attention to a number of additional enhancements.

Enhancements

"When love and skill work together,
expect a masterpiece."
— John Ruskin —

LOCATION

Location ... location ... location—it's everything in real estate and the same goes for trade shows. In many cases, however, an exhibitor's booth location is at the mercy of the show manager, especially if you are a smaller, first-time exhibitor. Often location is allocated according to seniority. This is usually interpreted to mean that you have the right of first refusal on your existing location up to a certain point in time. If you want a different location, then the show manager will decide according to a point system derived from a combination of the number of years at the show, the size of booth, sponsorships, and so on. However, if there is a choice, choose carefully. Your location in a show is an important element in your show success. Here are some things worth noting.

Your Objective

If your exhibiting objective necessitates interaction with visitors, then being close to the main entrance of a busy show may not fit the bill. While this may be advantageous from a visibility point of view, the sheer number of visitors in a high-traffic area may be counterproductive to your objective.

Booth Hardware

You have various options in terms of space configurations—islands, peninsulas, corners, in-line, and cross-aisle. Your choice of location may be limited by the type of booth hardware you have.

The general rule is that the more aisle exposure, the better, since it increases visibility as long as your booth looks like it fits in the space. Review your hardware before you make your final decision. While large island booths give you the most exposure, they are very expensive. You have to decide if the extra cost makes exhibiting sense.

Big versus Small Shows

The larger the show, the more critical the issue of location. In a smaller show of less than 150 booths, attendees can visit every exhibitor and still remain fresh, interested, and not feel overwhelmed. In a larger show, your booth runs the risk of being lost in the crowd. The larger the show, the more that care is required in choosing your location.

Your Competition

Some exhibitors see value in being placed close to the competition while others want to be as far away as possible. In some shows the decision is taken out of your hands by show managers who departmentalize their shows. From the show attendees' point of view, departmentalization makes a great deal of sense by simplifying decision making, since they can see all the exhibitors selling similar products and services in one concentrated area. The bottom line is that if your show is departmentalized, you will be close to your competition. If it isn't, then your visitors are likely to shop according to what is easiest for them.

Your Neighbors

There is nothing more disastrous than being across the aisle from a company that is clearly out-exhibiting you. A neighbor who has a dynamic booth can be a liability to you unless you have taken the time to coordinate your in-booth promotional efforts with theirs. A simple phone call to prospective neighbors often leads to better results for everyone. Simply, it gives you a chance to lesson the effect of competing for the visitors' attention.

Traffic Flow

In a normal trade show, attendees flow through one main entrance, get their bearings, turn to the right, and walk up and down the aisles. This does not necessarily mean that being at the entrance is the most advantageous. Your best spot is a place where there is a steady flow of traffic. Somewhere along the first few aisles on the right-hand side of the show are best. The farther you are away from the front door, the more attendee fatigue and information burnout you have to combat.

Areas to Avoid

This list is general with a few exceptions, but there are important points to consider.

- *Dead-end aisles*: The far corner of the exhibit hall can be a lonely place to visit.
- *Loading docks/receiving doors*: These locations tend to be noisy, and the stampede of other exhibitors trying to set up or tear down can be distracting. It can also be drafty, causing discomfort to you and your visitors.
- *Washrooms*: Although every attendee will visit these areas eventually, their thoughts are usually focused on something else other than the show.
- *Obstacles*: Many facilities have obstacles such as water pipes, fire equipment, columns, and pillars. These can present a real impediment to traffic.
- *Adjacent to a stage*: Unless you are sponsoring or participating in an event on the show floor, being next to the stage can be deadly. During presentations, attendees will have their backs to you and once the show is over, you will be overwhelmed by the stampede. Noise would also be a significant problem.

What If You Are Stuck?

If all else fails and you are assigned a space that is less than desirable, have no fear. The key to overcoming a location problem is to do whatever you can to bring attendees to you. The way to ensure that each attendee puts you on his or her "must-see" agenda is through an effective pre-show promotion program. (We will discuss this in greater detail in Chapter 7.)

PLANTS AND FLOWERS

Some exhibitors consider plants and flowers as frills that waste financial resources and take up space. If your exhibit space is very crowded, then you might want to skip the flowers and plants. However, flowers and plants will soften a harsh booth environment—a touch of color and live foliage often humanizes a display. The other consideration is attention to detail. It is true that your showstopper or big picture is the first thing that attracts visitor interest, but once they are engaged, they will start to notice the little things. Your attention to detail with the placement of a plant or vase of flowers conveys the message that you haven't forgotten anything and you are taking the show seriously.

You can purchase or rent plants and flowers. Review your exhibitor's manual to see if there is a florist service available. If not, check with the show manager to make sure that you can bring in your own or use an outside service provider. Plants are often hardier than flowers and are more tolerant of the harsh conditions of the show. Place your foliage at the back of your display. Traffic studies have shown that when plants are placed at one of the front corners, visitors tend to walk away from them to avoid brushing up against one of branches. If using flowers, avoid those with a strong scent like roses, gardenias, lilies, narcissus, carnation, hyacinths, lilac, phlox, or lily of the valley. Some visitors are sensitive or even allergic to certain smells and fragrances. It's better to be cautious and avoid overpowering smells.

HOSPITALITY

Hospitality can range from a plate of cookies or a bowl of jellybeans to lavish dinners with entertainment at exotic locations. There is no one answer that fits every exhibitor's budget and taste. While there is no rule that says without hospitality your exhibit will not do well, the Centre for Exhibition Industry Research reports that by adding hospitality to your mix, you can expect a 62 percent increase in converting visitors to qualified leads.

Hospitality comes from the word "hospitable," which is defined as "friendly, welcoming, and generous to guests or strangers." The Greek word for "hospitable" literally means "friend of strangers" or "fond of guests." In certain parts of the world, hospitality is not just a courtesy but also an obligation. If you are planning to include hospitality, you have lots of choices, but whatever method you choose, it has to be done professionally.

Some of your choices include in-booth hospitality, off-site events, sponsorship, or one-on-one entertainment. In a show setting, relationships are hard to build. Hospitality takes the visitor away from the noise of the show, offers a welcomed break, and helps develop a sense of trust when they do business with you. Every culture has its own interpretation of what is acceptable and what is not, but the one constant is food. Food is the great icebreaker. All religious, political, and social interactions revolve around food. Including a comestible element to your show plans is a perfect complement to the overall booth experience.

The discussion of all the cultural variables goes beyond the scope of this book. What one visitor may consider a delicacy another might find distasteful. Before actually embarking on your hospitality plans in a foreign market, you should check your local library or with a government official or local contact to ensure that your plans are consistent with what is acceptable in the local culture. You should also discuss your hospitality plans with your show organizer to ensure that you are not contravening show rules and to learn if there are additional fees payable to the manager or facility.

The next section offers an overview of various types of hospitality.

In-Booth Hospitality

In-booth hospitality can be as simple as a bowl of candy or a popcorn machine. However, a common misconception is that these readily available treats will attract lots of visitors. In fact, more often than not, visitors will grab a chocolate and keep on walking. Having a plate of cookies or cups of coffee on a table at the rear of the booth is a nice complement to the discussion. It makes your presentation more friendly and relaxes the visitor.

For food industry exhibitors, offering samples of food and drink is not simply hospitality but is also an opportunity for them to have visitors sample their products and provide feedback. As a result, exhibitors should create an appetizing display by cutting samples into small, bite-size pieces and arranging them attractively on a platter. While people are waiting for their taste, the boother has time to discuss some interesting facts about the sample.

Stand-Alone Hospitality

Stand-alone hospitality events are typically larger and require serious organization. One example is a hospitality suite in a local hotel or in the show facility to which you invite select visitors for an in-depth conversation. You may also consider a hospitality event such as a reception or banquet organized on one of the evenings of the show.

These larger events are not for every budget, but for those exhibitors who offer them, they become "must-attend" events at the show. Each year, there is a real pressure to outdo the previous year's performance. The most important consideration is to ensure that people come. This means careful consideration to timing and competitive events. It also means giving the right people the right incentive to come. The location can be a racetrack, library, train station, art gallery, or pub. As well as a unique venue, there has to be exciting entertainment and exceptional food and drink. Mediocrity simply won't cut it.

One-on-One Entertainment

It is popular and sometimes expected at international events. In Japan, for example, expect to host lavish dinners in nightclubs or restaurants that may last into the wee hours. In Taiwan, your meal may consist of twenty different courses. In Latin America while you might invite people for dinner, remember that their main meal is lunch, so dinner might not start until 10:00 or 11:00 P.M. If you follow this schedule day after day in a foreign country, after a full day at the show, you will soon be nodding off when they serve the soup. The cost of this type of entertainment can be staggering. On the bright side, one-on-one entertainment gives you a great opportunity to know your visitors better. While you might not be talking business during the meal, you will learn about their approach to life and how they view relationships. You have a great chance to lay the foundation and begin to build your long-term relationship with visitors, and that's what business is all about.

Promotion

An exciting venue, great entertainment, and delicious food will not guarantee a crowd. It all needs promotion that has been carefully and tastefully orchestrated. This can take the form of printed invitations sent by e-mail or faxed several weeks before the show with an RSVP, newspaper ads, inserts in trade magazines, invitations personally delivered during sales calls or at the booth, or VIP invitations offering preferred seating so your guests will feel special.

Since the invitation is a visual preview of the event, it must be presented professionally, printed on good-quality paper, well written, and appealing enough to warrant the visitor's attention. Including spouses on your invitation is always a thoughtful touch.

This advice holds true whether you are conducting in-booth hospitality or a stand-alone event. While many people will stumble upon your in-booth event, you want targeted visitors to include you on their "must-see" list. (See Chapter 7 for an indepth discussion.)

Other Hospitality Enhancements

Off-site greeters are crucial. Regardless of the number, quality, and position of your signs, some visitors will get confused. Your greeter should take the initiative to see if help or directions are needed. They should also be aware of other events that are taking place in the same facility so that they can provide directions to lost visitors. The other task of off-site greeters is to make a positive first impression. Often visitors' lasting impressions of your organization are a reflection of the first person they meet.

Roving hospitality agents should be strategically located throughout the reception area. They need to be constantly on the lookout for people when they first enter or those who are standing alone. Their job is to approach these people, introduce them to others, or direct them to the food and beverage area. At the end of the event, these same agents are located near the exit to thank visitors for attending and to help them find their coats, etc.

Badges and buttons are commonly used in many cultures. However, check this out carefully at international events since you don't want to insult people by asking them to wear stick-on name tags if they find them offensive. Also be aware that a pinned badge that goes through a silk dress or an adhesive badge on suede can cause permanent damage, so badges and name tags are optional for your guests but mandatory for your greeters and agents. Lanyard-held name tags that hang around the neck are commonly found at high-tech conferences.

Place cards are a great idea because they give you a chance to play "matchmaker" by choosing who gets to sits with whom.

Addressing guests is important. Your staff should never approach new people and address them by their first names. They should always address them more formally such as Mr., Miss, Mrs., Madame, Doctor, etc., until guests give them permission to use some other form of greeting. Such formality is very important at European and Asian shows. In North America, it is much less so.

DEMONSTRATIONS

Attracting attention at a show is a challenge. It takes a visitor approximately 3.5 seconds to walk by your booth. Since attendees are constantly being inundated with glitz, glamour, and a torrent of information, your challenge is to get them to stop at your booth. A show offers visitors an opportunity to experience products and services through all of their senses. Pictures are not enough. Imagine attending a car show and not sitting at the steering wheel or being at a food show without tasting the latest tidbits.

When visitors experience your products and services with as many of their senses as possible (sight, sound, touch, taste, and smell), their level of interest and commitment increases. Food show exhibitors allow their visitors to sample their products, computer exhibitors encourage their visitors to try out the new machines, and equipment manufacturers let visitors sit in the cab of their latest model.

A live demonstration is the best tool an exhibitor has to give visitors an experience and quickly grab their attention. Think back to your last visit to a consumer show. Of all those exhibitors, which do you remember? If you are like the rest of us, the answer was probably the exhibitor selling veggie cutters, Ginsu knives, or wonder mops. These exhibitors are masters at booth demonstrations, and you can learn from them. A demonstration with your products and services must be consistent with the image and professionalism associated with your organization.

The Centre for Exhibition Industry Rearch (CEIR) reports that what visitors remember most is good product information and a chance to see it in action. Whether you use dedicated presenters or your own exhibit staff (sales or product experts), a compelling in-booth demonstration is the key to the success of your overall exhibit.

The first myth to dispel is that demonstrations are only for products. Exhibitors of intangibles (services) often use this as an excuse for neglecting this important aspect of exhibiting. In fact, any product or service can be demonstrated. All that is required is an understanding of what is involved and a bit of creativity. As you read this section, you will learn the secrets to developing a winning demonstration whether you have a product or a service.

Demonstrations fall into two basic classifications—showstoppers and informational.

Showstoppers are the demonstrations you conduct near the front of your booth or in a dedicated section of your exhibit. They are usually more dynamic than an informational demonstration and often require presentation tools such as an LCD projector, plasma screen, microphone, and theater seating. They are designed to attract larger audiences and are general in content.

Informational demonstrations are usually conducted in a theater setting or a dedicated area of the booth away from the main traffic areas of the show. This type of demonstration is designed to give the audience more information than the showstopper. Demonstrations can last from five to thirty minutes depending on the space and setup of your booth. The longer the presentation, the more demanding your audience. They need to be seated comfortably and entertained. Often boothers or pre-show invitations are used to pre-qualify your audience so you can schedule these presentations at predetermined times throughout the show.

Attracting your Audience

Attracting attention means walking a fine line between tacky and professional. Exhibiting is "show biz," so a certain amount of chutzpah is necessary, but at the same time you don't want to put off the serious show attendees with whom you hope to establish long-term business relationships. You can draw attention to the beginning of a showstopper presentation more tastefully with eye-catching signage or helpful booth staff to direct traffic to the demonstration area. Some exhibitors have a countdown with bells chiming every ten seconds as the demonstration time approaches.

There are many tricks that you can use when the time approaches. If no one is standing around watching, the best thing to do is just begin. When planning your demonstration, it is important to have an exciting first few minutes, otherwise you will lose visitors' attention. The value of projected images is that you can create exciting and fun animation and sound to go along with your message. A little fanfare never hurts. Another trick is to have one of your colleagues stand watching the screen. This creates the impression that there is already some interest in what you are doing. A little action often creates reaction from the visitors walking by. Begin your presentation as if you had a full house and before long you will.

Audio Visual Tools

Today's audiences are pretty sophisticated, so that your presentation should be backed up by good quality sound and visual presentation technologies. There is a whole universe of audio-visual equipment and gadgetry to choose from. A professional audio-visual advisor can be of great help in selecting the right equipment for your use.

Audience Involvement

The beauty of an exhibition is that it provides visitors a chance to interact with you and your products or services. When planning your presentation, find ways to keep your audience involved. It doesn't have to be complicated, but it must allow visitors to experience the demonstration on a more direct level. Invite interested audience members to throw a switch, taste the chocolate-covered ants, hold a key element, touch the keyboard, and so on. The more you can get them involved, the greater their commitment.

You can also increase their involvement by using interactive games, quizzes, and questionnaires that they can complete while sitting or standing by a kiosk.

Another technique for piquing audience commitment is to offer them a memento for watching your entire presentation. This is beneficial on two levels. It gives visitors a reward of perceived value and it forces them to approach a booth person to ask for their prize. This is a good time for your boothers to gather pertinent information about visitors and feedback on your presentation.

What to Include in Your Demonstration

At an exhibition, the greatest challenge is dealing with visitors who have been overburdened with information by the time they get to your display. Your demonstration should give them enough information to understand what your product or service does and how it will solve their concerns without weighing them down with more information that leaves them stressed and confused.

Think about your presentation as an expanded television commercial. A television commercial has thirty or forty-five seconds to make an impression and leave the audience stimulated and excited enough to want to take the next step. There are two differences between a short television commercial and your in-booth demonstration: first, you have more time and, second, you can provide your audience with an experience. Let's look at both.

An in-booth demonstration can last from two to twenty minutes, depending on a number of factors. First, you need to have enough space to keep people comfortable during the demonstration and, second, you need enough valuable content so you don't waste your visitors' time.

Exhibitions are all about experience. The more senses you can tap into, the stronger your visitors' commitment. They need to see, feel, hear, smell, and taste your product and service. That's what exhibiting is all about—offering visitors an interesting array of sensory experiences. Demonstrations provide a wonderful opportunity to get the audience involved.

The Sizzle

There is an old adage in sales: "Sell the sizzle, not the steak." That is what a television commercial does and that is what your demonstration should attempt to do. It all starts with a clear understanding of your audience—their needs and perspectives. Every audience is different, so understanding the people you are presenting to is important. Earlier in the book, I outlined an important exercise for understanding your audience. This exercise helps you decide what information to include in a one-on-one presentation or in an in-booth demonstration. Having a clear profile of your customer or visitor will help you focus on your product or service's features and benefits that are most likely to appeal to your audience. This is a crucial point because there is a tendency to try and pack too much into a demonstration, thereby negating its value. To create a winning in-booth demonstration, follow these guidelines.

Define your audience: You now have a clear definition of your target audience. Rarely will one product be of interest to everyone, so focus on those who are most likely to grasp the benefits your product or service can deliver. (See Chapter 3.)

Define your objective: Your demonstration objectives are actually the shorter-term steps that will help you achieve your overall objective. For example, if your exhibiting objective was to get qualified leads, then your demonstration objective might be to attract quality people to your booth and spark their desire for additional information. If your objective was to create awareness, then you might try to boost traffic to check out your firm's web site for additional information. Stay focused on your exhibiting objective and find a shorter-term objective that can be accomplished in your demonstration that also complements your bigger picture. This shorter-term objective should also be measurable—for example, the number of people who ask for additional information, click onto your web site, talk to booth reps, sample products, or make purchases. (See Chapter 1.)

Define how you will achieve your objective: The question to ask yourself is "What do I have to include in my demonstration to achieve my objective?" This is not a list of the "nice to have's" but "must do's." From your audience's perspective, what is the crucial information you have to provide? Your "nice-to-have" list comes strictly from your perspective. It would be great to tell them everything, but remember, your "must-do" list is from your customer's perspective. It may take some time to focus properly. If you are unsure about what to include, ask your customers. Talk to a few satisfied users of your products or services and find out what is most important to them. Then build your demonstration around those features.

How to Tell It

To paraphrase Austin Powers, "This is show biz, baby!" The world's greatest chefs know that the best-prepared dishes in the world still have to be presented properly. This is the sizzle. If you can't do the presentation yourself, hire a professional to do it for you. Some people are naturals. They love the spotlight and shine when it comes to standing up in front of an audience. For others, it doesn't come naturally, but with hard work, they can learn effective platform skills and conduct exciting presentations. Then there is the third group who would choose root canal surgery over the torture of talking to a large group of strangers.

If you are in this last group, you can still overcome your fears and develop a great presentation style, but it requires a strong internal commitment. If you want to do it, you can. If you don't, bring in a pro.

Your demonstration script follows the same format you learned earlier in this chapter with one addition. A demonstration needs the element of proof, so tell them what you are going to tell them, tell them, prove it, and tell them what you just told them. No matter how good your platform skills, you need to prove your case.

Presentation Style

Get comfortable with the words: Political leaders have speech writers. So do business executives, entertainers, civil servants, and union representatives, to name a few. The trick to good speech writing is experience. The more one writes for the same person, the better a speech writer will be at getting the phraseology right. But seasoned professionals never present a prepared speech without first rehearsing it. During the rehearsal, they tweak the words here and there to ensure that each one works within their own unique style. The flow and credibility of their presentation depend on this.

Whether you write your own content for the demonstration or get someone else to do it, it is important that you are comfortable with the words. The trick is to read the script out loud. Reading it silently as you would a book is not the answer. Reading out loud gives you the opportunity to coordinate your mouth and your brain. Often there are words that look good on paper, but when you say them out loud, you stumble over them. Then there are words that feel uncomfortable and are just not you. Reading out loud gives you a chance to remove these troublesome words and replace them with words or phrases that work better with your style.

Get passionate about your products or services and their features and benefits: The toughest audience you will ever have to sell is yourself. If you can't convince yourself that you have a viable product or service or if you don't believe that your product or service will make a positive difference, then you are never going to convince anyone else. It comes down to honesty—if others believe that you believe in what you have to offer, then they are easier to convince.

The first step in convincing yourself is to gain first-hand knowledge by using the product or service. Take it for a road test, serve it to your friends and family, talk to your friend about it, play with it in your neighborhood, or share one with your golf buddies. Whatever you choose, "test drive" it in the real world. You may need to try it more than once. Emotions are strange, so give yours a fair chance. If you see (and feel) the benefits in your personal life, then you are developing a greater understanding of and appreciation for the product or service that you will be able to project in your presentation. If you can't convince yourself, your lack of commitment will give you away every time.

Be in the moment: No one cares if you had a fight with your spouse or too much caffeine and didn't sleep a wink, or if you are coming down with a cold. Demonstrating in front of an audience means that there is no past or future—only now. Focus 100 percent on your words and your audience—that's all that matters now. It's show time.

Rehearse, Rehearse, Rehearse

There is an old saying among professional presenters: "There are three things that make a great presentation—rehearse, rehearse, rehearse." All the great presenters and entertainers follow this advice religiously.

The purpose of rehearsal is to do more than ensure that you have memorized the script. It is your chance to get into the role of the demonstrator. Have you ever seen a performance where the entertainer started off slowly by building momentum and finally got into what he was doing by the end? In your demonstration you need to be on the minute before the demonstration starts. At an exhibition you don't have enough time for a warm-up. That's what rehearsal is all about. The more you rehearse, the more you get inside your script.

The words are comfortable, you know where you are going, you have worked out your timing, you are familiar with your audio-visual tools, you are comfortable with the physical setting, and so on. The more you rehearse, the closer to perfection you become.

However, don't think that rehearsal will help you get rid of anxiety. It doesn't. Some people get comfortable with public speaking quickly and others don't. Rehearsing in front of friends and colleagues is one thing, and conducting the demonstration at your booth with potential customers is quite another. If, even after countless rehearsals you still feel nervous, this is probably a good sign. Your nervousness is a form of creative tension that keeps you alive and in the moment. Use your nervousness—don't try to run away from it. Face it head on and you can tame it.

A rehearsal is best done in front of a live audience. After you have read your script to yourself out loud and feel comfortable with the words, you are ready to rehearse in front of an audience. The purpose of live rehearsals is not to show people a perfect demonstration but to find weaknesses and strengthen them. Both you and your test audience should understand this before you begin. You may choose to read your script first without audio-visual materials or you may jump into a full-blown presentation with all the bells and whistles.

Before you start, tell your audience what kind of feedback you are looking for. To be helpful, their feedback should be honest, positive, constructive, and specific. There is no point in sugar-coating feedback for the sake of ego. Remind your audience that you are depending on them to provide comments that will help you improve. It is important to listen without getting defensive.

It is also important to know what you are doing right. If you receive positive feedback, you have a chance to reinforce those things you did well.

Comments such as "That was pretty good" or "That was the worst presentation I ever heard" are not helpful. You need specific feedback. During your rehearsal ask your audience to take notes so that they can refer to specific words or actions that you can change in order to improve. Here are some suggestions for evaluating feedback.

First, you have to listen. Listening to feedback is difficult. People are saying honest things about your performance, and some of these things may not be pleasant to hear. Resist the temptation to get upset or to apologize. Simply say "Thank you" and leave it at that. Whether you agree with the feedback or not, write down all the comments so you can review them and incorporate changes into your presentation.

You may also choose to record your presentation. Afterwards, in the privacy of your office and armed with your feedback notes, review your performance. Now you can see what you did well and what needs improvement.

Revise your presentation and repeat this process as often as necessary. Remember the secret—rehearse, rehearse, rehearse.

COLLATERAL MATERIAL

There is a love-hate relationship between exhibitors and their printed collateral. Some exhibitors love it as a great way to avoid answering difficult questions or engaging in conversation. Besides, visitors crave it. Most brochures go unread. Somewhere between 85 percent and 95 percent will either end up in a landfill or in a plastic bag somewhere in a closet. Brochures require time and money to create. They take up space at the booth, and it's expensive to ship them from show to show. Think about the last time you attended a show as a visitor. What did you walk away with? If you are like most show visitors, the answer is a plastic bag, bursting at the seams with brochures and trinkets.

The trinkets you took because ... well, because they were free. You took the brochures because the product or service sounded interesting, you just couldn't say no, and ... well, they were free.

You return to the office with your trade show bag crammed with goodies. No matter how well intentioned your motives might have been about reading them someday, those catalogs, brochures, and price lists are now just a huge heap of litter. You are simply overwhelmed by too much information and have too little time to sift the wheat from the chaff, so you put away the whole bag. Now, as an exhibitor, your collateral materials are crucial. They are the medium for passing on the message about who you are and how you can help your visitors. It gives them details they need to make intelligent buying decisions and leaves them with an impression of what you care about and stand for.

Collateral materials are the best way to convey important messages to many people, but unless people read them, all that time, energy, and investment that went into their creation are wasted.

The straightforward solution to this dilemma is to present them more attractively. Brochures strewn over a table or piled high at the back of the booth are an eyesore and a waste of valuable resources. Yet your brochures can enhance your exhibit, encourage visits to your booth, and promote your products and services while delivering a clear, focused message about the fundamentals of your business. Although brochures are an important element in the booth package, it is also important to ensure that they are being read. First of all, collateral material encompasses traditional brochures, catalogs, sales sheets, price sheets, etc. Each item has value, but its value starts with you. Here are two winning strategies that will improve the ROI on your brochure investment.

Send Them Later

Take a few copies of each brochure and display them in a dedicated rack or holder. Avoid displaying your brochures horizontally as this takes up too much space. A better solution is to find a vertical freestanding literature rack, a countertop display, or hanging literature holders. These brochures should be clearly marked as "booth copy" or "display copy." Most visitors will respect this and will ask if they want something to take away.

When visitors stop and express interest in receiving some further information, all you have to say is "Rather than giving you more brochures to carry around, give me your name and address and I will have the materials sent to your office after the show," or "Leave me your coordinates and I will send you the information you need to access our web site."

This approach is a plus for most visitors who would rather not lug around bags filled with weighty materials. Then, when most of the other brochures collected at the show have been discarded, yours arrives with a covering letter thanking them for dropping by and offering to be of additional service. This puts you in a stronger position to reap some post-show business.

Encourage Readership

Not every visitor will be happy waiting for the material to arrive. Some visitors might want to come back to place an order or are busy gathering information to take back to the office for immediate consideration. You will assess each situation when you qualify the visitor (see Chapter 11). If you think that giving a brochure immediately is appropriate (although this will not occur in most cases), then you also want to ensure that it will be read.

But before handing the brochure to the visitor, there are two important steps to follow. First, print the visitor's name on the upper right-hand corner of the brochure. Many exhibitors simply staple their business card to the brochure, but this does not encourage the visitor to read it. The visitor's name on the brochure will stand out among the pile of literature collected at the show.

The second technique is to circle, with a thick marker, two or three benefits. This helps direct the visitor to the salient points you want to reinforce. If the visitor will make recommendations to a decision maker, this will help to focus his or her presentation. Since you will not be there in person, you can make this visitor your ambassador.

DRAWS

We have all done it—walked by a sign that read "Free Draw" or "Win a Free Widget," and deposited our business card into the bin. Draws are irresistible. There is no real commitment and maybe you can win something. Even Donald Trump has said, "Everything in life is luck."

Because of visitors' cavalier attitudes toward draws, exhibitors assume that they have no real value. However, a well-designed draw is an excellent tool for attracting booth traffic, especially for exhibitors who do not have enough space or staff to handle crowds. A booth draw catches visitors' attention, slows them down, and, if done properly, will bring visitors into your booth to talk to you.

Before setting up your draw, consider your objective for doing so. If your objective is to capture names for future follow-up, then providing a great prize will result in lots of names. However, be aware that most of these people will ask, "Did I win" when you call, and they won't remember you or your display. This approach may still have merit if the show was targeted properly and your need was to develop a database of industry people. However, for exhibitors who want a chance to talk to the visitors, the booth draw becomes an exercise in quality rather than quantity. If you are in this latter category, here are three points to consider:

1. *Your prize*: Ideally, your prize should relate to your company's products or services. Having a fantastic prize that everyone wants is not necessarily helpful. This means that you don't give away a new television unless you are Sony or Toshiba, a great trip unless you are American Airlines, or a motorcycle unless you are Harley Davidson. Make sure there is a connection between the prize and your organization.

    Your prize can be your product or service itself or discounts on future orders. Perhaps it is something that your customer will find useful in his or her business such as a library of technical books, advance copies of research reports, specific industry-related software packages, or a private luncheon with your CEO. It is up to you to be as creative as possible.

    Now, when some visitors walk by your booth, some will see the prize offered and say, "I'm not interested in that," and walk on, while others will find your prize valuable and stop.

2. *Ballots only*: It is easy for visitors to drop their business cards into a box and keep on walking, but when you require them to fill in a ballot, you are asking them for a time commitment. Your ballot should include some simple market research questions in addition

to the traditional demographic information. Some of these questions may include:

- How did you hear about our company?
- Have you ever used one of our tools before?
- Do I have your permission to keep you on our mailing list?
- What is your primary reason for attending this show?
- What other shows do you attend?
- What newspapers do you read?
- What trade magazines do you subscribe to?

3. *Talk to them*: It is not simply enough to have them enter your draw. Your final task is to engage these visitors in conversation. The booth draw is an enhancement that attracts attention to your display. To move to the next step, add the line "Must be validated by a booth person" to the bottom of your ballot. Now when visitors complete the draw ballot, it is up to the booth person to engage them in a conversation.

If you handle them correctly, booth draws work.

IN-BOOTH ACTIVITIES
There are many things you can offer in a booth to attract attention such as shoeshines, one-minute massages, putting greens, games, contests, and children's playgrounds, to name a few. In-booth activities take up lots of space and often the exhibitor is left wondering if they make sense. The short answer is a conditional yes, they do, in certain circumstances.

In-booth activities fall into three broad categories: entertainment, education, and games. The type of activity you choose should support your exhibiting objective. Each has its pros and cons, so implementation should be carefully orchestrated to ensure maximum impact.

Entertainment

In-booth entertainment is an opportunity to communicate a message in an informal, relaxed, and fun atmosphere (an interest zone 1 tool). It is an effective tool to use to attract attention to your display because in most cases you are making an emotional appeal to gain your audience's interest. Often visitors are inundated with information that's hard to absorb. Entertainment provides a welcome break from the information overload at the show. However, rather than distracting the visitor from the booth's objective, it can repackage information in a format that is fun, easy, and participatory.

In-booth entertainment can be anything from a stand-up magician to a complete floor show. It can include clowns, mimes, magicians, caricaturists, singers, drummers, jugglers, acrobats, and so on. Here are some guidelines for making your in-booth entertainment effective.

The message must be clear, relevant, and tailored to the audience. Whichever style of entertainment works best for you, it is crucial that the entertainment itself is customized to your unique needs. When engaging entertainment professionals, be sure they become well acquainted with the products or services you are featuring as well as your overall exhibiting objective. But let them choose the tricks, songs, or skits that best help you accomplish your objective while entertaining your audience. It is crucial that your marketing messages are integrated into the entertainment, otherwise there is no business value in it for you.

There are three types of entertainment suitable for booth performances: theater style, aisle, and roving. Theater style needs space within the booth. Aisle entertainment is a more typical approach in which an entertainer or group of entertainers is positioned strategically in the booth to attract the attention of people walking by. This could be a magician or a large ensemble. Roving entertainments can be clowns, magicians, or other people who wander throughout the show, talking to visitors, entertaining them, or giving samples. Some shows prohibit roving entertainment, so check with your show manager first.

Education

Visitors attend shows for a variety of reasons. One of the strongest is for education. Exhibitions are an ideal way for them to learn about new products and services, see new applications, or find out about new technologies and methods of increasing their own productivity. The same holds true at a consumer show where visitors have an opportunity to learn new skills that will improve the quality of their lives. According to a CEIR report, 26 percent said the amount purchased increased as a result of attending a seminar. Sixty-nine percent said they were more likely to make additional purchases within the next twelve months as a result of attending a seminar.

With this in mind, astute exhibitors have a unique opportunity. Whether you are exhibiting in a small booth or a very large one, there is always an opportunity to provide in-booth education in the form of a seminar.

The presentation itself has to be first-rate. Make sure it is not perceived as a sales pitch. Seminars are considered most valuable when the visitor gains relevant, applicable information. CEIR reports that 63 percent of all visitors attending in-booth seminars stated that attending seminars strongly influence their buying decision.

Seminars are different than demonstrations in their focus. The demonstration's focus is to whet the attendee's appetite for a product or service. The seminar is to give the attendees information that will help them improve their productivity.

Presenters need to be well prepared and rehearsed. If they give a sloppy, less than professional presentation, it will reflect on your entire organization.

Setting up an in-booth seminar should be done with care. In a smaller booth, you can get by with a couple of chairs. Your presenter will need a flip chart or overhead projector. In a larger booth, where you have the luxury of space, you can consider more elaborate audio-visual equipment and chairs. However, don't set out too many chairs. It is better to have all the chairs filled and visitors standing around watching, which creates the look of a crowded, popular seminar.

You may consider offering an incentive for visitors who watch the whole presentation. This could be a t-shirt, ball cap, samples of your product, or an opportunity to enter a draw. At one show, the exhibitor offered a crisp, new U.S. $100 bill. As you can imagine, every seat was filled.

In-booth seminars work. However, it is very disheartening to see a speaker talking to an all but empty booth. The key to a successful seminar, according to Barbara Siskind (yes, she is related), author of *Seminars to Build Your Business*, is in your marketing. "Marketing your seminar is probably the most important stage in your planning activities. ... Without a good marketing plan, nothing else happens."

You can publicize your in-booth seminar through newspapers and magazines, in the show guide, on your web site, by posting notices around the show (if the show manager agrees), mailing invitations to specific visitors before the show, including a flyer in the delegates' kit, or placing a sign in your booth indicating the times and topics of your seminars. For overseas shows, trade commissioners will often send out invitations to relevant companies in their database.

Booth seminars are a powerful way to attract attention to your exhibit. Once the seminar is over, your booth staff must be ready to approach visitors to offer any further assistance they need.

Games

Games are a broad category that includes both active (where the visitor gets involved) and passive (where the boother interacts with the visitor). Typically, games require less space than entertainment and education, yet can be a powerful attention-getter. Keep the activity short. You don't want to offer chess in your booth.

To encourage visitor participation, try active games such as a putting green, wheel of fortune, beat the champ race, or a scavenger hunt through the booth to get people to answer your questionnaire. Your game should interest people for a short time by keeping their attention focused on the activity. When it's finished, visitors should feel they have spent their time well. The game gives your booth staff the best chance of talking to the visitor to create a common bond and an easy way to take the conversation to the next step in the sales cycle. They are also great icebreakers, so if your boothers can link the game with your products and services, all the better.

Passive games hold the visitors' attention while some activity is being done to them. For example, you could offer back massages, shoeshines, or caricature sketches. They take only a few minutes to complete during which visitors are stationary and their thoughts are far away from the hurly-burly of the show floor. This creates a great opportunity for the booth person to strike up a conversation. In busy shows, such opportunities also arise while people are waiting in line for their turn.

PROMOTIONAL PRODUCTS

While walking through a show recently, I came across an exhibitor giving away Hula Hoops. You may remember Hula Hoops, an icon of the 1960s that you swung around your waist. This was a national show and most visitors traveled by air to get there. Have you ever tried to get a Hula Hoop through airport security? Do they even fit into the overhead compartment?

Candy is another popular giveaway. Many booths have bowls full of chocolates, jellybeans, popcorn, or Hershey's Kisses. They're not a bad premium if you are in the chocolate, jellybean, popcorn, or candy business. Will visitors remember your company if you do nothing but raise their cholesterol level?

Then there are exhibitors who give away bottled water, not that bottled water is not appreciated—it is. Tired and thirsty visitors need a refreshment break, but watch what they do with the bottle. They take it from your cooler, chug it quickly, and dispose of the bottle. What message do they take away?

The next time you visit a trade show, look at the giveaways. You will be intrigued by the scope and variety of things that exhibitors hand out. Then ask yourself this question: Do you remember who gave it to you? Is there some connection between the giveaway and the exhibitor's business?

Giveaways are of value only if you use them properly. Studies have proven that visitors receiving a tangible reminder of their visit to your booth retain a better feeling about you than other exhibitors who leave them empty handed. So, while premiums work, it's important to give them some lasting value. For your next show, consider some of the following ideas:

- Avoid cuteness. Although cute is important, there should be more than that to a good promotional product. It needs to connect with your corporate image and marketing message and should reflect the product or service you offer. Your promotional product supplier can take you through the process and help you choose what is right for you.
- Put your name and contact information on the item. What is the advantage of having a cool item that says "ABC Company" and nothing else? Add your web site or 1-800 number. Make it easy for the customer to contact you later.
- Make it convenient. Remember, visitors need to get back to the shop and you want to make sure your promotional item goes with them.
- Display them properly. The front counter of your booth is not a good spot. It only encourages "grab-and-run" collectors who want free stuff but have no interest in doing business with you.
- Don't use them as an incentive to attract people into your booth. "Hi, do you want a free digital watch?" Who could refuse?
- Use them as a tool to help you disengage when the conversation is over. It becomes a tangible way of thanking people for their visit. Remember to point out your contact information so the visitor knows that this is more than a free gift; it is also a helpful reminder.
- Choose compact items that don't take up too much space. You don't want to clutter your booth with boxes of promotional items that take attention away from the real reason you are at the show.
- Choose promotional items that the decision maker will use, not their children.

SPONSORSHIPS

Event sponsorships are additional opportunities to connect with your marketplace beyond your display to influence changes in visitor perceptions and behavior. We have all been affected by sponsorships from large banners at the entrance of an exhibit hall to program inserts. Sponsorships have evolved into a crucial component in any exhibit manager's arsenal of marketing tools. Today sponsors' expectations are much higher than just placing a banner at an event. Sponsorship programs are now part art and part science, combining several marketing disciplines and activities to make a sustained impact with the intended audience. The CEIR reports that booth efficiency, that is, its ability to attract quality visitors, increases by a whopping 104 percent when sponsorship is included in the exhibit plan.

Further research shows that sponsorship investments can range anywhere from 15 percent to 25 percent of an annual marketing budget, making it an increasingly important and accountable component. With this increase in accountability comes increased pressure to demonstrate a positive return on investment.

How Shows View Sponsorships

From a show's perspective, when an exhibitor buys into a sponsorship program in addition to their exhibit space, they open the doors to a whole new world of collaboration. Sponsorships can range from comprehensive branding programs and speaking opportunities (e.g. sponsoring a celebrity to speak at a show or an internal company spokesperson) to show floor traffic building.

When a company includes sponsorship in their exhibit plans, they send a clear message that they are a serious supplier seeking to differentiate themselves from their competitors. In return, they get access to benefits not normally available to the masses. For example, a trade show sponsor is more likely to be included in a pre-event news release highlighting features at the show or will be referred by show management for an interview during the event. They are also more likely to be considered for a seminar topic or industry panel in the event's conference program.

Determining Value for the Sponsorship

One of the biggest challenges is determining a value for a sponsorship offering. In a trade show environment, considerable time and resources are spent attracting a qualified buying audience. Exhibitors should expect to pay a premium for their sponsorship to access this audience. Trade shows attach a tangible value based on the quality of the audience. In a typical consumer-related event, the value of the sponsorship is usually attributed to *cost per impression*. This can range from a few cents to many dollars. Because the audience is more likely to be broad-based, organizers must show good overall value for audience reach. Another aspect that drives sponsorship pricing is the level of demand for the sponsorship. One of the most common requests is the opportunity to speak in front of a qualified audience at an event. Since speaking opportunities are generally limited and many exhibitors want the opportunity, the premium for such opportunities is generally high and is usually attached to a more comprehensive sponsorship package.

Negotiation and Implementation Techniques

With a disciplined approach, every exhibit manager can be successful at negotiating and implementing an effective exhibition sponsorship program. Here are some useful tips.

1. *Articulate what you want to achieve from your trade show sponsorship*: With the myriad of sponsorship options available at a trade show, you need a clear focus on your objectives to narrow down your choices. For example:

   • If you want to position your company as *subject matter experts*, consider sponsorships that include a speaking opportunity.
   • If you want to *introduce a new company name or product*, look at an event sponsorhip package that includes a multitude of mass branding vehicles (e.g., ads, banners, e-mail broadcasts, etc.) or specific items such as show bags or name-badge lanyards that all visitors receive.

- If you want to *promote an event-related workshop*, consider sponsorships that allow you to communicate pre-show messages to potential visitors through pre-show registration materials.
- If you want to *generate booth traffic*, consider sponsorships that place an offer (e.g., coupons) in the hands of all visitors.

2. *Work closely with your show manager*: Your show representatives need to have a thorough knowledge of the opportunities that are available throughout the event so they can help you choose the right sponsorship.

   By sharing your marketing objectives with the organizer and asking him or her for advice and recommendations, you are not only tapping into the organizer's expertise, but also effectively engaging the organizer to help solve your problem.

   It is important to remember that show organizers want exhibitors to be successful because it's good for the long-term health of the event. However, it is also prudent not to take everything they say at face value. Do your own homework.

3. *Compare the cost of the sponsorship with that of other vehicles to reach the same audience*: Once you've identified the appropriate sponsorship vehicle, it is important to assess the value and expected ROI to ensure that the money well is spent. The key question to ask is "How much would this cost to do on my own?" For example, if you were able to distribute 10,000 pieces of literature through a sponsorship, compare the cost of the sponsorship against the cost of an updated database, envelopes, mailing house fees, and postage.

   When assessing the value of the sponsorship, you must also assess the intangible value of proper timing, the prestige of the event, and competitive factors.

4. *Negotiate the exhibit space and sponsorship together as a package*: When you negotiate your exhibit space and sponsorship at the same time, you leverage your investment. The reality is that once you sign the contract for your space, the show organizer's

incentive to "cut you a deal" on the sponsorship is sharply reduced. Focus on the total investment your company is willing to make on the show.

The negotiating stage is the ideal time to ask for value-added benefits. When negotiating these benefits, the odds are that you'll have greater success if you ask for "throwaways" that cost no or minimal dollars for the event to deliver. Examples include extended exhibitor listings, a logo block alongside your listing in the event guide, web site links, or new product listings. The key is to ask because if you don't ask, you will never receive!

5. *Tie sponsorships to the show floor*: For many exhibitors, this is sometimes the hardest to achieve because effective integration of sponsorships with the exhibit program takes time, creativity, and a disciplined approach. There are several advantages to integration. It reinforces your message with visitors (multiple impressions), makes it easier for them to find you on the show floor, and helps them remember you after the event.

    Basic approaches to integration include ensuring consistency in printed materials and signage. More complex approaches include tailoring your booth activities to tie into your show message. For example, if you were an event management firm introducing a slogan, "We add spice to your corporate events," you might consider a sponsorship that includes distributing a coupon for visitors to redeem at your booth for a bottle of kitchen spices. The important aspect to remember is that exhibit/sponsorship packages are ideal opportunities to display some creativity. Make sure your investment pays off and that you stand out from the rest of the crowd.

6. *Build in performance measures*: No one has money to burn. You must measure the effectiveness of the sponsorship against your show objectives. Once again, this requires out-of-the-box thinking and discipline. The following are examples of how performance measures can be built into sponsorships:

- Code the document (e.g., VIP call-in number, a web site password) to determine how many responses were generated through the promotion if you are distributing literature with a post-show call to action.
- Measure a booth traffic-building sponsorship by providing coupons and recording the number of visitors taking advantage of the show offer.
- Conduct periodic exit surveys to see if visitors remember your promotion.

By making performance measurement part of your sponsorship strategy, you will develop a clear understanding of what motivates the audience and what works best.

7. *Be an implementation fanatic*: Remember, when implementing your sponsorship program, you need to stay on top of each deliverable to ensure that you are getting full value for your investment. No matter how experienced the show organizers are, they are still managing multiple tasks; consequently, things can fall through the cracks. To stay on top of all the changes and new demands, you need to work closely with your representative during each phase to let him or her know that you expect flawless execution.

   Proofread all print copy and signage before they go to press. If you continuously monitor each opportunity, you may find additional leverage. For example, if you have an ad in the event guide as part of your sponsorship, contact your rep just before the publication date to review placement and ask if there are any unsold premium positions. If there are, and it is a matter of slotting one of the existing ads into that position, that simple call could increase the value of your ad by as much as 50 percent.

8. *Evaluate*: A post-show review of your sponsorship is important to determine ROI. In addition to conducting an evaluation of tangible benefits, ask your colleagues for their opinions to get a well-rounded view of the sponsorship.

Sponsorships are a natural extension to your exhibiting activities. Choose correctly and the results can be spectacular.

IN CONCLUSION

There is more to a display than looking good. To be successful at exhibits you need to carefully understand a multitude of components that make up a good display. If we were to leave the discussion here, it would be like having a party and forgetting to send out the invitations. Now we must do everything possible to make sure people come.

Pre-Show Promotion

"A wise man will make more opportunities than he finds."
— Francis Bacon —

You might think, "I've got a great show manager who does extensive pre-show promotion. They spend lots of money attracting the right people to the show, so all I have to do is sit back and wait. They will come, won't they?"

Show management's responsibility is to promote the show and bring a qualified audience to the door. They will talk about the exhibitors, special features, associated events, timing, and location. They create the hype.

Your promotion, however, is for a different purpose, so relying on show management to do your job is a mistake. The best that show management can do is deliver a crowd of qualified people, but they cannot guarantee that every attendee will go to your booth—that's your job.

The Centre for Exhibition Industry Research reports that 76 percent of attendees come to a show with an agenda. They have already decided whom to see and what events to attend. The purpose of your pre-show promotion is to secure a place on their agenda.

INVITATIONS

One of the most effective pre-show promotion tools is sending out a formal invitation to drop by your booth to see new products or services. To make your next pre-show invitation a winner, here are a few tips:

- *Invite a targeted group*: Identify those attendees who fit your customer profile. Your list can include current customers and prospects provided by your sales force, targeted names obtained from your association, last year's delegates, or through a list broker.
- *Be creative*: You need to ensure that your invitation will be noticed and remembered. Consider sending your invitations in a bottle, guitar case, popcorn bag, book, tubes, or decorative wrap—something that will grab the attention of the people you want to impress. Invitations that appeal to the gustatory sense go even further. These may include custom-made chocolates, gingerbread cookies, or a bottle of vintage wine. The bottom line is that you want to be noticed, remembered, and, most of all, get people to visit your booth. Show business starts long before the show opens.
- *Tie-in with an attendee pass*: Many show organizers offer special passes, whether they are VIP or discount coupons or a pre-registration form. Include it with your invitation.
- *Include an incentive*: Attaching a ballot with instructions such as "Bring this ballot to our booth for a chance to win a great ... " or "Bring this invitation to our booth for a special gift" will do the trick.
- *Color-code your invitation*: If differentiating your prospects is helpful, then send each group an invitation in a different color. Then when the visitor approaches the booth, your staff will immediately know what to do or which gift to give.
- *Doing it once is not enough*: Sending a reminder by fax a week in advance, and an e-mail two to three days before the show, will greatly increase the rate of redemptions. Have your sales force hand-deliver invitations to selected people when making sales calls.
- *Count your results*: Have your booth staff keep a tally of the number of invited guests who come to the booth and record their comments. It is also helpful to know which prospects did not respond to

your invitation. This is the best way of assessing the impact of your invitation and the effectiveness of your target list. It's also your first step to making changes to future show plans.

- *Focus on the shopping need*: The CEIR reports that attendees are attracted to a show for three major reasons: career development, general awareness, and shopping. According to the CEIR, shopping is the main purpose for most attendees and should therefore be the focus of your pre-show promotion. Unless you have a pre-determined focus in mind, knowing what attracts your audience can provide a powerful insight into their motivation. The three charts that follow reveal the details of each of these needs.

REASONS FOR ATTENDING—CAREER DEVELOPMENT	
Item	*Average importance (Scale 1–7, with 7 being very important)*
See new technology	5.7
Personal development	5.5
Better job performance	5.3
Recharge motivation	4.7
Networking	4.6
Hands-on experience	4.5
Meet other users	4.3
Learn about regulatory issues	4.3
Seminars	4.2
See what large institutions are doing	4.2

Source: CEIR report AC32

REASONS FOR ATTENDING—GENERAL INDUSTRY AWARENESS	
Item	*Average importance (Scale 1–7, with 7 being very important)*
Insights into industry	5.3
Build relationships with exhibitors	4.7
Anticipate what product designers are thinking	4.6
Prospect for suppliers	3.7
Name recognition by peers	3.7

Source: CEIR report AC32

REASONS FOR ATTENDING—SHOPPING NEEDS	
Item	*Average importance (Scale 1–7, with 7 being very important)*
New product introductions	5.9
Examine products	5.8
Idea generation and planning	5.7
Information about existing products	5.3
Compare brands	5.3

Source: CEIR Report AC32

When you average these needs, the clear winner is shopping. For a good deal of your visitors this will be the most significant reason for them attending and therefore it should be the focus of your pre-show promotion.

REASONS FOR ATTENDING—AVERAGE IMPORTANCE	
Item	*Average importance (Scale 1–7, with 7 being very important)*
Career development	4.7
General industry awareness	4.4
Shopping needs	5.6

Source: CEIR Report AC32

The bottom line for exhibitors is not just to build your exhibit and hope for the best, but to invite visitors and watch them come.

PUBLIC RELATIONS

Public relations can give your exhibiting effort a tremendous lift. The media—such as trade magazines, consumer newspapers, television, radio, or electronic media—can help you throughout the show cycle. Before the show, they inform potential visitors of new and interesting products and services that they should not miss. At the show, through trade dailies or on-site distribution of publications, the media keep visitors up-to-date with last-minute show-related news. And after the show, their stories about newsworthy events or an overall summation of the show tell people what they missed or remind them of what they saw.

The first step is to identify the media you wish to approach. Your show manager can be of assistance here. Most shows will actively pursue media attention, so they may have media lists with contact names for you to use either on your own or as part of their media efforts.

The next step is to develop a list of targeted media contacts. Here are some of the typical people you will meet:

- *The editor* is typically responsible for the overall content, style and look of the publication.
- *News editors* are responsible for what is covered. Their decisions are based on timeliness, interests to readers, and relevance.
- *Features editors* usually supervise stories and feature articles, which provide extended coverage of a topic.
- *Correspondents* are either staff or freelancers who do the actual writing.
- *Reporters, picture editors, photographers, cameramen etc.* take care of a variety of specialized media functions.

Finding the right person to pitch can be a challenge. One technique is to follow your media closely and take note of who is writing about what. When you are planning your public relations, try to contact the right person with whom to discuss your ideas. Give them a "heads up" before you send them a media release.

Your relationship with the media is crucial. Don't wait until you need them to make contact. Nurture your relationship with relevant updates and make yourself available for background information.

Writing Your Media Release

Be careful to avoid making your media release look like a sales pitch. The media is not interested in selling you. If your media release sounds too commercial, it won't work. Look at it from a journalist's point of view—is your story of interest to the reader? Are you providing some new information or facts about the reader's world? Can you shed some new light on an important issue? Do you have a solution that will help make the reader's life or business more productive and profitable? These are the kinds of questions a journalist will ask, so think of the answers ahead of time. This "hook" is the key to a successful press release. Now you can develop the contact.

- *Create a strong heading*: A good strong heading is what the media read first. If you can capture their attention quickly, there is a chance they will look at the balance of the release as well. If your heading is boring, uninteresting, and irrelevant, they will discard it.
- *State the conclusion first*: This is the opposite of traditional report writing where you build your case and draw it together with a conclusion. The media need to know quickly where the story is going. Ensure that you answer at the beginning the questions: who, what, why, when, and where.
- *Keep the style appropriate to the publication*: If you are preparing a press release for a general interest magazine or a newspaper, then your writing style should be sharp, direct, newsy, and informative. If you are writing for *Scientific American* or a technical journal, you need to add more details.
- *Add quotes*: Quotes from industry experts, studies, reports, and statistics add tremendous credibility to your pitch. The more your statements are backed up by reliable third parties, the more credible your claims will be.

- *Keep it short and concise*: Your release should be one or two pages, double-spaced.
- *Timing is everything*: Send your materials in a timely manner. Ask about deadlines and ensure that your materials arrive when the media wants them. Do not send them in advance. If they arrive too far ahead, they will be forgotten. Ask, listen, and respond.
- *Provide further information*: At the end of the release provide contact information. If the media call, return their calls promptly. Delay in returning the call for a day or two when the media are on deadline means that you will be left out.
- *Date your release*: Every release is time sensitive. Identify the date of your release and indicate if your exhibit ties into other industry or seasonal events.
- *Include a booth visit incentive*: If you want the media to visit your booth, then you will have to entice them. You can lure them with promises such as: meet our CEO; test drive our new product today; get your photo taken with …; or attend our hospitality reception.

Prepare Your Media Kit

In addition to the media release, your kit should include additional facts and statistics, product brochures and sales sheets, samples of recent published stories, awards, background information about your organization, a sample of the product (if practical), photographs (high-resolution images can be burned onto a CD), and any additional details you think the media will need to tell your story properly. Then put the whole media kit in a glossy presentation folder or other attractive packaging that makes it interesting and convenient for the media to carry back to the office.

Many large shows have a media room where members of the press congregate. Often individual exhibitors can have their media kits displayed in this area. Check with your show manager to see if this is possible.

A small supply of media kits should be kept at the booth so that your staff can give them out to media representatives on the show floor. Then be sure to follow up with your media contacts through periodic phone calls or e-mail reminders.

The Press Conference

Consider organizing a press conference for major announcements. This involves arranging a suitable location, getting notices out to the media mentioning the time and place, offering some hospitality, arranging for the necessary audio-visual equipment, and having a briefing paper to hand out at the end of the press conference. Often the media room host can help with this function, but remember that press conferences are for really big industry news. If the media do not view it that way, they simply won't show up.

ADVERTISING

When you buy advertising space, as long as you get your copy in on time and pay your bills, the advertisement will appear.

All the media outlets that you approach for public relations are also open to paid advertising, albeit it in another department. Look for opportunities to capitalize on an existing advertising campaign. Rather than booking a stand-alone show ad, you may be able to stretch your budget with co-op ads by adding banners or inserts on existing advertisements.

WEB ANNOUNCEMENTS

Check with the show organizer about linking your web site with the show's site. Links might also be available through your suppliers. Prior to a show appearance, create a banner ad on the home page of your web site so your customers can see where you are exhibiting. Then create a show page to list your whole show schedule and some of the special features you will have at each.

OTHER PROMOTIONAL IDEAS

The challenge and fun of promoting an exhibit is finding new and interesting places that attract the attention of your audience where they least expect it. Here are some notable ideas:

- Wrappers or inserts on the official show guide
- Wraps over the headrests of local taxis

- Your company's name and booth number on the reverse side of taxi, restaurant, theater, or hotel receipts
- Hot-air balloons coasting over the show facility
- Company trucks parked strategically and conspicuously in local parking lots
- Your company's name and booth number on escalators in the show facility or official hotels
- Your company's name in lobbies of local buildings, elevators, or washrooms
- A sandwich named after your company and offered by a local restaurant during the show.

Creating a display is only part of your challenge. Getting visitors to spend time with your staff is another. A good show promotion plan will help generate the kind of traffic you want.

IN CONCLUSION

Developing a great plan and a winning booth and not promoting your attendance will put your entire investment at peril. Promotion is a crucial part of your event planning. Now that everything is in place, we come to the challenge of managing your most important resource—people.

PART THREE

Managing the Human Resources

*"You cannot be a success in any business
without believing that it is
the greatest business in the world."*
— Thomas Watson Jr. —

The Pre-Show Briefing

"Knowledge is the only meaningful resource today."
— Peter F. Drucker —

Do pre-show briefings really matter? The Centre for Exhibition Industry Research (CEIR) reports a 68 percent increase in converting visitors to qualified leads when a company takes the time to train its staff, so, yes, it does matter. If a bit of human resource preparation produces such a staggering increase in qualified leads, one wonders why everyone doesn't do it. Some typical excuses I have heard include: "I don't have enough time and it's difficult to get everyone together," or "My booth staff have been doing shows for years." Some comment that their staff feel resentful about being at the show in the first place and a briefing is just an added burden.

Take a moment to look at how much money you spent last year on exhibiting. This is not just the cost of renting space at a show but all the costs, including the booth, shipping, literature, travel, preparation, opportunity costs, and so on. When you add it all up, the number will surprise you. Now, what was your return on that investment?

Whatever those results were, you might see a 68 percent improvement by adding a pre-show training session that takes as little as one hour. The pre-show briefing can be conducted by someone in your organization or by an outside exhibit consultant. The advantage of the latter is that often the consultant comes with a built-in credibility that internal folks can't command. It's not that the internal people don't know what they are doing, but sometimes they are viewed as being too close to the situation.

Which of these statements is true?

1. Informal pre-show training will increase your booth staff's performance.
2. Booth personnel who receive no training at all are more likely to perform better than those who received some informal training.

The obvious conclusion is that some training is better than none. But, if your answer is number one, you're wrong. According to a study by Tanner and Weilbaker for the Centre for Exhibition Industry Research (CEIR Research Report EC1, June 2000) untrained staff were more likely to "greet attendees more quickly, ask more questions and were more likely to close the sale" than those who had received some informal training.

While few experienced exhibitors will dispute that the make-or-break element of any show is the booth staff, more often than not, their overall performance leaves much to be desired.

So, if improved booth performance is the goal and informal training doesn't seem to do the trick, what factor affects staff behavior positively? Could it be the attitudes of the attendees, some characteristic inherent in the staff chosen to work at a show, or is there a third element such as the type of training?

ATTENDEES' BEHAVIOR

Tanner and Weilbaker observed three types of trade show attendees and their effects on the booth staff:

1. The passive buyer who avoids making eye contact while meandering down the center of the aisle.

2. The curious buyer who will approach a display and examine its products, signs, and graphics.
3. The active buyer who is more assertive and will walk into a booth, touch the products, observe the demonstrations, and ask questions.

If you were working a booth, which type would you most likely approach? Common sense might suggest that the active or curious were more likely to be approached than the passive. After all, if an attendee avoids eye contact and expresses very little interest, the chance of rejection is great. Surprisingly, the study concluded that "more than 90 percent of all buyers were approached by booth staff irrespective of type."

BOOTH STAFF PERSONALITY

Conceding that attendees' behavior has little influence, Tanner and Weilbaker turned their attention to the personality styles of the booth staff. Perhaps, they hypothesized, certain personality traits are the key to improved booth performance.

Tanner and Weilbaker used the social styles model to test this hypothesis. Social Styles categorizes people into one of four observable styles: amiable, analytical, expressive, and driver. Here some differences were noted.

Researchers examined booth staff as they asked questions, made product and rapport-building statements, and closed the transaction. They found that the expressive were more likely to ask questions and close the transactions than the amiable. However, when it came to product and rapport statements, there were no significant differences.

While personality types somewhat affect booth behavior, there was no significant difference to conclude that this is the key factor to improved booth success.

THE THIRD ELEMENT: THE TYPE OF TRAINING

When we dismiss these first two factors (attendee behavior and staff's social style), our attention turns to the type of training as an answer to improving how staff handle themselves at trade shows.

The researchers found that those with informal training were "slower in initiating conversations with attendees resulting in fewer sales than staff without any type of training." Formally trained staff, on the other hand, were more likely to engage attendees in conversation and close the sale. Rapport-building and product statements were also more prevalent with formally trained personnel. There are a few reasons for this.

Informal training often lacks the specificity required for a successful show appearance. Most managers and booth staff are poorly equipped to handle the unique selling environment at a show. They assume that traditional selling skills are all that's needed. Often informal training is nothing more than providing new product information with very little help in developing strategies to handle trade show crowds. Moreover, informal training is often not viewed with the same seriousness and commitment as formal booth training.

The obvious conclusion is that formal training (versus informal training) has more impact on staff behavior at a booth than does the attendees' attitudes and staff personality types. The bottom line for anyone wishing to improve show results is either do the job right or not at all.

Here are the elements to include in your pre-show briefing:

1. *Show description*: Familiarize your staff with the show amenities, layout, timing, location of key exhibitors, and special features such as seminars, keynote addresses, press conferences, and hospitality. We often take this information for granted, but to the untrained eye, shows can be overwhelming and difficult to maneuver.

   In addition to show activities such as seminars, hospitality and industry events, and keynote speakers, there are other extracurricular activities that will make your staff's time at the show as stress-free as possible. These include such things as staff dinners and spousal programs.

2. *Your quantified exhibiting objectives*: Your boothers need to know their purpose, otherwise they are simply putting in time. You

should articulate your exhibiting objectives and let each boother know how he or she should achieve them. You can divide the overall booth objectives by the number of boothers, hours, or shifts. Then allocate the portion to that time frame. Keep in mind that there will be some times when there are lots of visitors and others when traffic is slow. Giving everyone an equal portion of the overall show objectives would be putting some boothers at a disadvantage. Be fair and realistic when setting individual expectations.

In Chapter 1 you learned the importance of setting individual objectives. This briefing is a great time to help all boothers find opportunities to gain experience at the show that will be of benefit to them personally.

3. *Booth overview*: Be sure to include new features, troubleshooting, location of supplies, emergency contact information, and details on how to maintain the look of the display, as well as details about in-booth demonstrations, seminars, draws, giveaway items, handling of literature, and lead-retrieval technology. Whether your booth is 100 square feet (9 square meters) or many thousands, boothers need to familiarize themselves with the logic that went into the creation of the space.

4. *Booth staff schedule*: Don't leave the booth schedule to chance. All boothers need to know specifically when they will be working at the booth and when they are free to pursue other show activities. A typical booth shift should not exceed three hours. This is difficult work and staff need time away from the display to refresh themselves and relax. If there is only one person working the booth and the show is eight hours long, there is no magic solution that will make the day easier. However, if you have the resources, a break every three hours is ideal.

Often company representatives, administration, or senior staff want to drop in and see how their company is doing. It's nice to have them in the booth as it is a great opportunity for them to build their sense of pride in the organization, but, whenever possible, ask them to restrict their visit to a scheduled time or when the show is slow.

5. *Conduct a review of the expected attendees*: In Chapter 3 you created a list of the visitors who are likely to attend the show and their reasons for attending. Share this list with your boothers to help them get ready to handle the traffic. This is also a good time to review scheduled appointments with key decision makers or to remind your staff to be on the lookout for other key people who need to be handled carefully.

6. *Understand staff's strengths*: Staff should also let each other know their area of expertise so that when one of these key people shows up or if someone asks a technical question, each boother will know who to consult for information.

7. *Booth skills*: This last item is the one often left to chance. Successful boothers understand that their skills must be honed to this unique environment where time is a scarce commodity. Booth skills follow the same principles as ordinary sales skills with an emphasis on the challenge of limited time. Boothers must understand that it all starts with their ability to control the outcome of every interaction.

   The following is a summary of the four steps to include in your pre-show briefing. These steps are covered in depth in Chapters 10 through 13. Make sure you incorporate each step.

SUMMARY OF THE FOUR STEPS TO EFFECTIVE BOOTHING

1. *Breaking the Ice* (Chapter 10)
   • Develop approach questions
     - Ask open questions
     - Focus on business
     - Don't ask a question if you don't want the answer

- Don't ask a question if you don't know what to do
  with the answer
- Don't ask a question that leads to a pitch

• Develop questions in the three scenarios
  - When a prospect approaches the booth
  - When there is a demonstration or sampling
  - When nobody stops at the booth

2. *Gathering Information* (Chapter 11)
  • Develop questions in the six ACTION criteria
    - Authority
    - Capability
    - Time
    - Identity
    - Obstacles
    - Need

3. *Making Effective Show Presentations* (Chapter 12)
  • Opening: Tell them what you are going to tell them
    - Bridge from information getting to information giving
    - Restate the visitor's wants
    - Articulate the next steps

  • Body: Tell them
    - Review concerns one at a time
    - Introduce features, benefits, proofs, and confirmation
      statements
    - Bridge to next want

  • Close: Tell them what you just told them
    - Review concerns
    - Ask for the commitment
    - Reinforce rapport

> 4. *Disengage* (Chapter 13)
>   • Presumptive disengagement
>   - Refocus
>   - The setup
>   - The propositions
>
>   • Conciliatory disengagement
>   - The acknowledgment
>   - The invitation
>   - The reality check
>   - The call to action

Your pre-show training should focus on mastering this four-step process. But just because you describe these steps, don't assume that staff can use them. They need time to integrate them and that comes through practice. The more they can practise these new skills, the more proficient they will become. Include this practice time in your briefing. And don't forget to talk about follow-up. Studies have shown that nearly 80 percent of all leads generated at shows are mishandled. With your follow-up plan in place, you can be assured that each show lead will be treated appropriately.

This may sound like a lot to pack into a one-hour presentation, so be selective. Some of these points can be covered in pre-show memos, during regular staff meetings prior to the show, or a special show briefing held at the show location. The choice is yours, but remember that when booth staff are in a strange city or situation, they need as much help as possible.

The cost of adding a pre-show briefing is minuscule compared with the benefits you will realize. Make sure this small step is included in your show plans for your next show.

IN CONCLUSION

Working at an event is not something most people do everyday. It is a strange and sometimes hostile environment. Your pre-show briefing is one of the best investments you will make as it introduces your staff to the information they need to thrive, and at the end of the day they will know that they have accomplished something important for their employer and for themselves.

The Four Stages of Boothing

"The successful person is the individual who forms the habit
of doing what the failing person doesn't like to do."
— Donald Riggs —

"Excuse me," the customer called out in desperation, "would some-one please help me?" The cry interrupts a group of employees engaged in lively conversation. One member of the group looks toward the customer and says, "Oh, I didn't see you. Can I help you?" Sound familiar? At a retail store it's poor business behavior. But at a trade show, where the competition is a stone's throw away, this type of behavior will lead to lost business and credibility.

Managing the human component can be a daunting task. You are faced with a number of challenges:

- Commissioned-based salespeople often resist taking time away from their territory to work at a show.
- Staff who have participated in shows before may resist adapting their behavior to the time-pressured environment of a show.
- There may be a human resource shortage that forces you to work with anyone you can get.
- Your personnel pool may consist of people who are technically proficient but do not see themselves in a sales role.

• There may be limited time, money, or corporate desire to implement a staff training program.

Before you think that managing the human element is a good idea but
impractical to implement, remember that *everything* depends on the
people in your booth. Without them, nothing will work. It's like
building a computer without the software to run it.

Working a booth is really not for everyone. To succeed you need
stamina, patience, skills, and an understanding of what makes a good
boother.

Your staff must understand the need to change from their usual
work style in order to work in an environment where everything happens faster. That's what exhibit marketing is all about. The good news
is that people at the show come to you. The bad news is that even
though you know they might arrive sometime during the show, you
don't know exactly when or if they will arrive one at a time or all at
once. The CEIR reports that the average number of sales calls a person makes out in the field daily is 2.7. Multiply that by five days a
week and fifty working weeks each year and you get a total of 675
calls. This is assuming that you didn't take a sick day, your car was
never in the shop for repairs, and you took no statutory holidays. Six
hundred seventy-five calls! At a well-chosen trade show or event, that
many people can walk by your booth in the first couple of hours.

The next time you work at an exhibit, do the math. Take the total
number of expected visitors and divide this number by the number of
exhibit hours. Then divide this number by sixty. The result is the
number of people you can expect to pass by your booth every minute
on average. And don't forget that this bit of arithmetic is only to make
a point. There is really no such thing as average. Every show or event
has its own unique traffic patterns. There are busy times and quiet
times. If you subtract the quiet times from the busy times, your number gets worse, so keep the math simple.

Let's create a hypothetical two-day show with eight exhibiting
hours each day where you might expect 5,000 people. Your math
would look like this:

$5,000 \div 16 = 312.5$ per hour
$312.5 \div 60 = 5.2$ per minute

In this example you will have your annual quota of 675 calls walk by your booth in one hour and twenty-nine minutes.

In an environment where you have to deal with so many people in such a short amount of time, clearly a change to your approach is appropriate. Let's backtrack for a minute. Imagine that you are meeting with one of your 675 calls in a normal business environment—their office, your office, a showroom, etc. What would your conversation sound like?

It should include information about the client, his or her needs, and the business solutions the client is looking for. It would also include information about your products or services and how they will help the client solve some issues. Then, if you are like 99 percent of the rest of us, the conversation would be sprinkled with seemingly non-related topics such as the weather, kids, vacations, sports, hobbies, etc. Why?

Think of a first meeting with a new prospect in your normal (non-show) environment. Your conversation probably revolved around the prospect's needs, your products or services, and lots of social chit-chat. No conversation is complete without talking about the weather, sports, current events, kids, politics, movies, holidays, or the traffic. You include the social chat because your ultimate goal goes beyond the initial sale. Your focus is on developing a long-term business relationship. You search for commonalities between you and the prospect—the more things shared in common, the stronger the bond and the greater the likelihood for business.

Essentially, your job is to connect with people and to begin or continue building long-term relationships. Salespeople who ignore the potential that these long-term relationships afford and focus only on their short-term needs are wasting valuable time. For them, every day becomes a new challenge void of the advantage of repeat sales and referrals. However, developing a solid business relationship built on trust and comfort ensures an ongoing relationship, post-sale contact, new business opportunities, referrals, and testimonials.

At a show the quest for long-term business relationships is the same. From your point of view you want the business. You want the prospect to take advantage of whatever you are offering and continue to do so in the future. From your prospects' point of view, there is a real sense of satisfaction (and comfort) in dealing with people they trust and for them, it makes shopping easier. They will go back to the person who treated them well because it is easier than starting all over again.

People buy from people they like, people they trust, people with whom they feel rapport. And since most of us are interested in long-term business, rapport is crucial in developing clients we can do business with in the long run. When there is this feeling of trust, the chance of ongoing business increases. When rapport is ignored, the result is often constant haggling about money and terms instead of focusing on relationships and problem solving.

In ordinary non-show business situations, we have the luxury of time. But at an exhibit, as in our example above, every minute you spend with one person means you are losing the opportunity to talk to 5.2 others. Clearly there is a need to hone your skills to compete in this time-pressured environment.

So, why do some exhibitors succeed while others do not? Why are some booth staff unable to make the transition easily from everyday business methods to show business? The answer is straightforward. Many people assume that making the adjustment to the show environment is easy. In fact, it is difficult and requires time and training. Good boothers tend to evolve through four stages of growth. Good boothers are made, not born. Let me explain.

STAGE 1: ENTRY LEVEL

Stage 1 boothers who are attending their first show do not realize that the situation requires them to adapt their behavior. Boothers behave reactively by standing at the back of the booth and waiting for attendees to ask a question, rather than taking the risk by approaching proactively. They are often engaged in paperwork, talking on their cellular phone, huddling with colleagues, reading the newspaper, or browsing company literature—in short, any activity that helps them cope with the long hours of the show without having to talk to anyone.

Stage 1 boothers answer questions; they never ask them. The reality is that many attendees will not always make the first move. Some, of course, will, but many won't. They may be timid, shy, uncertain about what to ask, not sure how the product, service, or program will meet their needs, but most of all they suffer from information overload and don't want to be bombarded with more irrelevant information.

For those courageous visitors who actually ask questions, the stage 1 boother offers only basic information that leaves the visitor who had a serious question with incomplete details of questionable value.

Why do stage 1 boothers act this way? They have never had an opportunity to learn the right way to interact with visitors at a show. They have chosen or been told to go to a show with no preparation. Stage 1 boothers lack purpose. They work without the benefit of an objective.

Try this experiment. The next time you attend a show or event, walk toward the first booth you see and note how you are treated. If you get into a conversation, ask the boother why he or she is at the show. You will probably get answers such as "My boss sent me," or "I was the only one available," or "It gave me a chance to combine some R & R time on my company's expense," or "I really don't know."

If a boother knows his or her role and has the skills to accomplish that role, we would never see a stage 1 boother again, which brings us to stage 2.

STAGE 2: BETTER BUT STILL A LONG WAY TO GO

Stage 2 boothers have advanced slightly, but still have a long way to go. They often view the show as an extension of their showroom or retail store. It is easy to spot stage 2 boothers, who are usually casually dressed and look unprofessional as they stalk attendees like hunters in search of prey while invoking timeworn lines such as "Hi, can I help you?"

Then when the unsuspecting attendee says, "yes," or asks a question, what follows is a lengthy discourse that includes the details of every feature and benefit of the product or service.

Stage 2 boothers tell everyone the same thing. Ask for some information about a certain product and you are sure to hear the same pitch the previous visitor heard. Attendees come to the show to find out how products and services will work for them. A canned pitch will not serve everybody.

The stage 2 boother can also be found handing out brochures to attendees passing by the booth or, worse yet, sitting behind a table placed strategically across the front of the booth. Stage 2 boothers use games and premiums to attract attention: "Hey, wanna win a set of golf balls?" Who could say no?

Why do people work at stage 2? The first reason is a lack of comfort. We all have a zone of comfort. In a business scenario, it is comfortable to do the tried and true—that is, talk about your product or service to one customer at a time. Repeating this over and over develops confidence. When something changes—say, the potential of talking to hundreds of people who pass the booth—the result is extreme discomfort. Research has shown that one of the biggest social fears is the fear of talking to strangers. So what do inexperienced boothers do? They resort to the comfortable and familiar—pitching. The second reason why some boothers are in stage 2 is because they lack clear direction and skills. Stage 2 boothers have some sort of objective, but it is vague at best. Refer back to Chapter 1 where you learned how to set objectives. At stage 2, boothers have not been given the advantage of clear, quantifiable objectives. They were told just to "create awareness" or "collect leads." To do their job properly, boothers need more details.

Whose fault is it that people tend to work trade shows at stages 1 and 2? The employees' or management's? The answer is both. Managers need to set clear, motivating show objectives, and staff have a responsibility to ensure that they know what is expected of them.

If each of your booth staff were told "Your objective is to find four qualified leads and here is how we define a lead," they would ask, "How do you expect me to accomplish that objective?" By asking that question, they immediately propel themselves into the next level of proficiency—stage 3.

STAGE 3: THE FIRST SIGN OF REAL IMPROVEMENT

It was a short step from stage 1 to stage 2, but progressing to stage 3 produces the first really dynamic improvement in results. Stage 3 boothers hone their skills and work efficiently in the trade show environment with an appreciation of the importance of a focused objective. Remember, stage 1 boothers had no sense of purpose whatsoever and stage 2 had an objective that was vague at best. At stage 3, the problem is solved.

Objectives differ from show to show. Booth staff's reason for being at a show may include one or more of the following: to obtain orders, find qualified leads to work with after the show, introduce new products, open new markets, create an image, introduce a new product or service, gather competitive intelligence, conduct market research, or create media attention. In fact, there are more than 100 legitimate reasons for exhibiting (see Chapter 1). Knowing their primary objective and being able to achieve it in a measurable and realistic way is one of the key characteristics of a stage 3 boother. If the objective is sales, how many sales are expected? If it is to recruit dealers, how many dealers should they recruit? If it is to introduce a new product, to whom should they introduce it? Having a measurable and realistic number enables your booth staff to know clearly what is expected of them.

Stage 3 boothers also have had all their questions answered. In Chapter 4 you learned about management's responsibility in conducting a pre-show briefing. During this briefing your staff had their questions answered. They are no longer strangers to the show but welcomed participants.

Now the stage 3 boothers are ready to develop the skills necessary to achieve their stated show objectives. Booth skills are compartmentalized in the four parts of the information-gathering process: approaching, information gathering, presenting, and disengaging. Each of these skills will be explained in detail later. It should be evident that once they master the information-gathering process, the quality of results improves dramatically. Boothers are now ready to reach beyond their initial grasp into the master's level of booth staffing—stage 4.

STAGE 4: WHERE REAL RESULTS ARE FOUND

Stage 4 is where a dramatic improvement to the trade show investment becomes possible. Those who use stage 4 booth skills do some key things that those at stages 1, 2, and 3 do not. Stage 4 booth staff go beyond approaching, information gathering, making the presentation, and disengaging. Stage 4 boothers take a radical turn.

Ask yourself this question: Why would anyone want to do business with you and your company? Your first answer might be better quality, great service, good reputation, and the best price in town. But think a bit harder. Assuming that your product or service is of good value and your competitor's product or service has merit, the factor that will tip the scales in your direction is your ability to relate to the customer—to develop rapport.

Stage 4 boothers know that there is not enough time at the show to treat visitors the same as they might if they were in a non-show environment. The challenge of rapport building at a show is a lack of time. At stage 4, boothers fit their rapport-building skills into the unique environment of a show setting. They will develop the flexibility of dealing with every visitor individually and leave him or her with a real desire to want to continue the business relationship after the show. And, more important, the boother will achieve a huge increase in trade show results and have some fun being there. Later in this chapter you will learn more about the rapport-building process, but for now, know that those who work at stage 4 clearly have the competitive edge over their stage 1, 2, and 3 counterparts. Stage 4 is where real show rewards are found and boothers' well-developed objectives are met.

THE SKILLS

Working at stage 4 is analogous to taking part in a play with four acts. The four acts are the skills of approaching, gathering information, presenting, and disengaging that all stage 3 boothers have mastered. Add rapport-building skills and the result is a stage 4 master boother.

Each act requires unique techniques that blend together in one harmonious play from start to finish. Your staff are the stars of this play. Their actions determine how the other players respond. Stage 4 boothers know that the sign of greatness is when they can convince the other actors—the visitors—that the play is about them and not the boother. When this happens, an Academy Award is only a heartbeat away.

Time is the enemy when working an exhibit. The goal is to take control of time by working through each act masterfully. The end of one act cleverly segues into the next. The four acts blend into one elegant dialogue between the stage 4 boother and the visitors, and through it all, rapport builds gracefully. Before we continue, it is important to meet the other players.

THE SIX PEOPLE YOU ARE
LIKELY TO MEET AT A TRADE SHOW

Edgar Dunn

In Chapter 3 you learned the importance of clearly defining your target market. You created a thumbnail sketch that best describes the person who will help you reach your exhibiting objective. Edgar is that person.

Edgar has a real and immediate need for your product or service. He is ready to make a decision that is compatible with your sales cycle, and has the authority and the resources to act.

Edgar wears many disguises. The trick is not to let Edgar fool you by his clothes, grooming, or personal style. Pre-judging Edgar based on his nonverbal behavior leads to lost business opportunities. Once you have identified Edgar, treat him well—he can become your friend for life.

Emma Hope

Emma and Edgar look and act the same. She has a need for your product, service, or information. She is in a position of authority and has the resources necessary to implement a decision, but here's the catch—Emma is not ready to make a commitment now or anytime within your sales cycle. Something is holding her back. If you can find out what it is and deal with it properly, you will witness a metamorphosis as Emma becomes Edgar. Every good businessperson has had situations in which he or she has converted an Emma into an Edgar, but you are at an exhibit. Be careful, Emma can be devious. Without your awareness, she will steal from you your most precious commodity—time. Remember, working at an exhibit is not like working in an ordinary business situation. Every minute you spend with someone who does not fit into your carefully defined target diverts your attention from the real prospects. Every minute another 5.2 attendees cross your path. Could one of them be a real Edgar that you have missed?

Emma has long-term potential, which is better dealt with after the show when you have more time.

Louis Fatale

Emma has a close cousin named Louis. Louis is an amiable fellow who shows a keen interest in your offering. He nods his head in agreement, says all the right words, and is willing to listen to anything you have to say. Sound too good to be true? Remember the old saying: "If it seems too good to be true, it probably is."

The bottom line is that Louis lacks potential. He can't use your offering now or anytime within the foreseeable future. Louis is commonly referred to as a "tire kicker." He has a genuine sense of curiosity about new and interesting things. He has an insatiable appetite for information whether it is meaningful to him or not. He learns for the sake of learning. He talks for the sake of talking.

Ally McMate

Ally is a sensitive person. Her temperament is a learned response. She has met many boothers who have simply rebuffed her and assumed that just because she doesn't make the final decision she has no worth, so Ally has her back up.

Ally is like the sleeping tiger. Wake her up abruptly and she will attack, but give a gentle nudge and Ally can become a great friend who is willing to help you in many ways. When you talk to Ally, you learn that there is a need for your product or service and the resources are in place. What is missing is the authority to act. Ally is not a decision maker. She is still a valuable friend because she can get your information to the right people, spread the word, or give you names to follow up.

Zelda Post

Zelda asks lots of questions. Stage 1 boothers love Zelda because the questions keep them occupied, but the reality is that Zelda has an ulterior motive—employment.

Trade shows are a rich quarry of potential employers. For those in the job market, walking through a show can save countless hours of frustration sending unsolicited resumés or answering advertisements that attract hundreds of applicants. So, armed with her questions, she approaches.

Moe Lassis

Moe is the last of our players. Moe comes in many disguises. Moe can be the spouse of a delegate, someone coerced into attending the event by a friend, a fellow exhibitor, or simply someone who doesn't get out much. Moe has a need for human contact. Moe is filled with riveting stories about everything from troubles with his kids to opinions about world leaders. In spite of Moe's many persona, what they all have in common is their ability to talk incessantly. They drone on and on and on. In the company of Moe, time slows to a crawl.

MOTIVATE THE DOERS

If senior managers do not support a trade show strategy, the best of plans become corporate orphans passed along from manager to manager with no one taking any serious interest. However, commitment from junior and middle management is just as crucial. These are the folks in the trenches who deal with the day-to-day challenges of planning, organizing, and executing a trade show strategy. What motivates them?

While money and job security are genuine motivators, with the prospect of layoffs looming everywhere, the promise of job security is nice, but is it realistic?

A successful show is more than following the rules and hoping for the best. It requires each team member to work at an above-average level of involvement. It means pushing the creative boundaries and working out of the box. It means a level of excitement and enthusiasm seldom seen in other parts of the corporate culture. So, how do we motivate the doers to perform at this level?

There is no one answer that works for everyone since what excites some will have no effect on others. Knowing your staff is the first crucial step. This is easily accomplished by doing a bit of research. Talk to the key players and get their opinions. Elaborate incentive programs do have value, but they are often geared to salespeople and ignore the people behind the scenes. More often than not, it is the little things that are most meaningful. Consider some of the following:

- *Let them see the big picture*: Show them how the show fits into the overall marketing strategy.
- *Get them involved early*: Planning should start at least three or four months prior to a show, or even earlier if it is an international show.
- *Give them adequate time*: Each member of your team already has full-time responsibilities. They may require additional help with their added workload.
- *Let them know their work is important*: A short note or a quick phone call to say "How is it going?" or "Good job" goes a long way.
- *Make them feel part of the team*: Plan some team activities. A project launch or a post-show celebration will do the trick.
- *Communicate to the whole team regularly*: Let everyone know everything and encourage ideas.
- *Encourage feedback*: Get your staff out of the "Not my department" syndrome. If one person has ideas or advice for another, he or she should be encouraged to offer it freely.
- *Listen*: This is not as easy as it sounds, so when one of your team is talking, stop and listen.
- *Let them get involved with all aspects of the show*: The educational programs as well as other industry activities are a terrific way for people to develop their potential.

- *After it's over*: Publish pictures of your booth and your team in a company newsletter or special bulletin posted on your intranet site. Hold a post-show bash as a reward for a job well done, or have everyone get together for a debriefing and dinner.

Motivating the doers is not rocket science. We all need to know that the work we do is important and appreciated. So, if you don't have any more money to put into the pot, try a little TLC. You will be amazed at the results.

IN CONCLUSION

Now that all the players have been identified, the play can begin. Your job is to identify which player you have encountered and adjust your response accordingly at a stage four level of boothing. You are now ready to learn the skills.

Breaking the Ice

*"One starts an action simply
because one* must do *something."*
— T.S. Eliot —

Some visitors will approach you at a show, but as often as not, they resist making contact. Why? Attendees have their own agenda. Some visitors will scope out the whole show before they commit to a detailed look at specific exhibits. Others may feel awkward and fear their questions might be simplistic or dumb. Sometimes attendees are confused about your display and don't immediately see the benefits you offer. Still others may view your booth staff as unapproachable. Some attendees are simply shy while others fear they will be pressured into placing unwanted orders.

Booth staff should remember why they are at the show. Whatever their objectives, they are in the booth to do business. At an exhibit you have to be proactive—you will waste valuable opportunities if you let the prospect walk by.

Approaching strangers isn't easy. For many it is the number one social fear. They have to overcome their timidity, develop an effective opener, avoid closed questions, and focus on business, all while overcoming the chief objection visitors have about booth staff—that they are too pushy. Some staff may feel comfortable being proactive with people one-on-one in their offices or on the showroom floor. But being proactive at a show can be terrifying. Staff may fear being rebuffed or appearing pushy or simply not know how to approach gracefully. They need to reframe their thinking and look at approaching as a compliment—an attempt to engage visitors that, nine times out of ten, they will appreciate.

A good opener not only engages visitors in a meaningful conversation about business, it gives boothers control over the situation. Meaningful conversations are those that allow a smooth transition from the first act to the second. Ask the first question and the answer will form the beginning of an effortless bridge to the second act.

The best openers are questions that are carefully crafted to get the conversation going. The best questions are those a boother can ask smoothly and honestly. Henrik Gibson once said, "Each bird must sing with his own throat." Your boothers' effectiveness will be diminished if he or she is not comfortable with the questions. Each boother should create his or her own opening questions.

There are two do's and three don'ts that boothers should consider when creating their approach questions.

DO #1: ASK OPEN QUESTIONS

Effective openers invite the visitor to pause and continue the conversation. For this reason, closed questions— those that can be answered with a simple "yes" or "no"—will not be as effective as well as questions that require a lengthier answer. Open questions usually begin with words like "how," "what," "when," "where," and why.

DO #2: FOCUS ON BUSINESS

An open question is better than a closed question, but not just any open question. Asking about the weather or the local sports team may invite a conversation, but this conversation will not move the boother any closer to an objective. Effective openers do not waste time. They get directly into the job of qualifying visitors. The best way to start is with a question around their needs.

In choosing a theme for your exhibit, you will have focused on a key benefit of your product or service. Having boothers question the visitors' need for this key benefit is the most effective way to launch into conversations.

Here are a couple of examples:

- "How often do you run into problems transferring business information from program to program?"
- "How are you keeping up with the rapid changes in technology?"

DON'T #1: DON'T ASK A QUESTION IF YOU DON'T WANT THE ANSWER

Openers such as "Hi?" or "Nice day, isn't it?" are timeworn and ineffective because they do not go anywhere. Visitors can answer with one word and keep on walking. Or, worse yet, they can answer at great length and waste a boother's time with irrelevant chitchat.

The worst questions to ask are those that have no meaning. How often have you walked a show floor and heard, "How are you doing?" What's your answer? You probably said "Fine," and moved on. The problem with asking questions about the attendees' health or the weather is that most of us don't really care about the answer. We think openers like this are a friendly way to start a conversation, but they are boring and insincere. Why not test this out? The next time you visit a show and someone asks how you are doing, stop and tell him or her. You will quickly notice a blank stare in the person's eyes as he or she pretends to be interested in your health challenges. In fact, he or she is more interested in talking to other prospects who are walking past the exhibit.

DON'T #2: DON'T ASK A QUESTION IF YOU DON'T KNOW WHAT TO DO WITH THE ANSWER

I frequently hear that seasoned salespeople have an incredible ability to think on their feet. After years of experience, they feel inhibited with prescribed lines and prefer to rely on their instincts to deal with the situation at hand. This is valid in normal business situations where there is lots of time, but at an exhibit it's different. Don't use show time to be creative; use it to meet objectives. The best booth performers have a well thought-out approach. By thinking about the questions ahead of time, they can plan a response. Remember that there is no guarantee that the attendee will give the expected answer and boothers don't want to be caught off guard.

A boother once approached me with the question, "Are you familiar with our company?" This was a good approach question, but when I answered "yes," he was dumbfounded. He didn't know what to say. Apparently he wanted me to say "no" so that he could bounce into his well-scripted pitch, which leads to the third don't: Don't be caught without an answer.

DON'T #3: DON'T ASK A QUESTION THAT LEADS TO A PITCH

Show visitors suffer from information overload. They are inundated with information as they attend the seminars, watch demonstrations, and walk by booth after booth. Eventually nothing more can sink in. The offer of more information is the last thing they want.

Boothers really don't know what kind of information visitors want. Ignoring this rule is tantamount to asking "Hi, do you mind if I give you a whole bunch of information you may or may not care about?"

Avoid questions such as "Do you want to see our new widget?" or "Would you like to hear the ten reasons why most users run into problems with their servers?" This is too much information.

Ice-breaking questions help reveal players' identity. Their answers to boothers' questions will give them the first clue. Staff need to be careful not to pre-judge visitors based on the way they look, dress, or talk. They should approach everyone as if he or she were the most important person in the world.

A good approach doesn't have to be complicated. In fact, it should consist of words that can be used comfortably and honestly. Studies have proven that up to 93 percent of a visitor's impression is based on *how* questions are asked rather than the actual words used. When questions are asked that show genuine interest in the person, the questioner is perceived as a caring, interested person.

THREE ICE-BREAKING SCENARIOS

To begin crafting ice-breaking questions that work, it's best to understand the various times they are required. At a show, boothers encounter three typical scenarios. Being prepared for each is the key

When a Visitor Approaches the Booth

When a visitor approaches and appears interested in a product, graphic, or something in the booth, the boother has an open invitation. Finding a business-related opener comes from focusing on whatever attracted them in the first place. "What have you heard about our new widget?" or "How do you deal with the challenge of cash management?" or "What caught your eye?" or "What attracted you to our booth?" The trick is to keep questions simple and non-threatening. All approaches should be preceded by the booth person introducing himself or herself.

"Hi, my name is Barry Siskind. What interested you in my display?" or "What have you heard about this product?" or "What has your experience with this product been?" or "I'm not familiar with your organization. What do you do?"

When There Is a Demonstration or Sampling

The real purpose of the demonstration is to attract many people to your display. Sampling is an opportunity for visitors to try out a new product. Once the demonstration or sample has been given, ignoring visitors is like watching business stroll in the other direction. Savvy exhibitors understand this, so when the demonstration ends or the sample is given, they will ensure that the interested visitors are brought into the exhibit for a more in-depth conversation or they will use the opportunity to gather additional information.

There are two ways to conduct the demonstration:

- *Situation 1*: Boother A works the exhibit while boother B conducts a demonstration or handles the sampling.

- *Situation 2*: Boother A conducts the demonstration or gives the sample himself or herself.

Let's look at each in turn.

Situation 1

If the demonstration or sampling is going well, it will attract a crowd. Clearly the demonstrator will not have time to talk to all interested parties. Here is where the additional help is needed. As the demonstration or sampling is drawing to a close, boother A's job is to spot one member of the audience who might be interested in additional information. Spotting individuals with an above-average amount of interest is easy.

Visitors express interest in a number of ways. Some do it verbally with positive comments and questions. Others do it nonverbally. They nod their head, lean in closer, or smile. Experience will be the best teacher when looking for positive interest.

Once the demonstration or sampling is over, boother A approaches and asks, "What part of the demonstration was most applicable to your needs?" or "How does this product fit into your work needs?" In the case of sampling, ask, "How does that compare with the product you are using now?" or "What reaction would you expect when you serve this to your family?"

Don't forget that each approach is preceded by the boother introducing himself or herself.

Situation 2

During the demonstration or distribution of samples, boother A takes note of which participants express an above-average amount of interest. Stopping and giving this person undivided attention is a mistake. The reality is that boother A doesn't know the interest level of the remaining visitors. Boother A needs to keep the attention of the interested person while completing the demonstration or sampling. The best method of achieving this is to get the interested person involved.

People attend exhibits to experience products and services with as many of their senses as possible. By getting the interested person involved in the demonstration or sampling, their need to experience your product is being met. When developing the demonstration or sampling, your audience involvement is an important factor. Allow people to touch, taste, smell, see, and feel, for example, by holding the product or touching a keyboard. It could be giving someone a freshly baked goodie or asking someone to flip a switch. Interested people can assist in handing out samples. The greater their involvement, the greater their commitment. Once the demonstration has ended, ask this person, "How do you see using this technology in your workplace?" or "How would your guests react if you served this at your next party?"

When Nobody Stops at the Booth

The most difficult challenge is when the exhibit is quiet and visitors are not coming to the booth voluntarily. This scenario breeds bad habits in booth staff such as slacking off, making phone calls, talking to colleagues, or taking a coffee break. Staying focused on their objectives is the key. Even when the show is slow, the boother's job goes on. If visitors are not coming into the exhibit, boothers should position themselves on the perimeter of the booth and look approachable—smile and relax. As people walk by, staff should try to catch their eye. As many as 95 percent of visitors will ignore booth staff, but once someone does make contact, staff need to be prepared with a simple opening question such as "What are you looking for at the show?" or "What's the best thing you have seen at the show so far?" or "How receptive is your family to new dinner ideas?"

This third situation may be the most difficult. It may be difficult at first, so encourage your boothers to be patient. It takes time to master the art of approaching visitors who are simply walking by.

At this point, boothers don't know if they are talking to Edgar Dunn or one of his five compatriots. However, the ice has been broken and they can now proceed to information gathering.

One final word. Now that you understand the importance of approaching visitors, help your boothers develop and practise simple approaches. They may not be successful the first time. Coach Casey Stengel once said, "Most ball games are lost, not won." It takes time to perfect any of the skills in this chapter. With time, proactive approaching gets more comfortable and new lines can be added to the mix. Practice makes perfect. At an exhibit your boothers can't be anything but perfect.

IN CONCLUSION

If you have done your job well, a meaningful conversation has started. Your job is now to find out as much about this prospect as possible in a short period of time. That's what information gathering is all about.

Gathering Information

"Many strokes, though with a little axe,
hew down and fell the hardest timber'd oak."
— William Shakespeare —

The ice is broken and the conversation has begun. The visitor may have answered with probing questions related to your product or service, or may have given vague answers, or perhaps began an oration that seems to lead all over the map. The boother's next job is to gather enough information to determine how to spend the rest of the time with this visitor. If the boother chooses to go on to step 3, which is the presentation, he or she needs to know what to present. If the boother chooses to skip step 3 and go immediately to step 4, the disengagement, the staff person had better be right about this prospect. Boothers don't want to lose good opportunities because they pre-judged the visitor.

Gathering information is at the heart of the cycle. The reason boothers spend time doing this is threefold.

1. It gives boothers valuable insights on how to allocate their time.

2. It confirms to visitors that their needs have been understood. Research has shown that nearly 40 percent of all visitors will leave a booth without making any sort of commitment because they

felt the booth person had not taken the time to understand their needs. Good probing questions let the visitor know that the boother cares enough to take the time.

3. It opens up post-show opportunities. It tells boothers how and when follow-up with this particular prospect is to be accomplished.

In the first few moments of the interaction with visitors at the booth, *don't tell them anything*. When boothers choose to jump into a presentation, they don't know what the prospect wants to hear. They don't understand the visitor's unique perspective. They don't know what outcome the visitor is striving to achieve. Therefore, instead of jumping prematurely into a presentation, they should take the time to gather key information about the visitor's situation.

During this time boothers should not be *information givers but information getters*.

Gathering information is a matter of taking ACTION, an acronym for six bits of information that are crucial to the stage 3 and 4 boother's performance. The following six steps are generic. They are a broad approach to gathering information. As you proceed through this chapter, think about the information that is crucial to your situation. Sometimes the six steps work well as they are, and sometimes they need to be modified. Use the ACTION format as a template to create the questions your staff needs to ask.

The order of the questions is unimportant. Often when one question is asked, the visitor will give information related to other questions. Repeating a question becomes redundant. Don't feel constrained by the acronym; use it as a tool. The value of acronyms is that they are easy to remember and in the heat of the interaction with a visitor, boothers need tools to keep them focused. The ACTION acronym is one such tool.

If the exhibiting objective is sampling or testing and you know the demographics of the visitors, gathering additional information might not be useful. If you are not conducting a post-show follow-up, having this information may not be of value. In this case I recommend picking a question or two that will help reinforce the value of your sample such as "Have you used this type of product before?" or "This is the newest offering from the ABC Company designed to reduce your cholesterol intake without sacrificing taste."

While boothers will vary the order of their questions to accommodate the conversation, here are some examples of the information that can be uncovered.

A = AUTHORITY

One of the six bits of information that booth staff need to know is the visitor's level of authority. Is this visitor Edgar Dunn or Emma Hope with the authority to make a decision, or perhaps Ally McMate who can influence the decision? It is important for staff to know which of the six players they are dealing with. Authority is one clue. Remember, boothers need to gather enough information to make a decision about what to do next.

If boothers choose to make a presentation, then it is important to ensure that they use the right words. For a decision maker, the conversation will focus on getting the decision made. For the decision influencer, the conversation will center on the visitor's ability to get the information to the right person. In either case it is important to say the right thing to the right person. When a visitor is misread and the words are wrong, there is a serious impediment to building rapport. Think about your own situation. Perhaps there was a time when an overzealous salesperson spent lots of time telling you about the advantages of making a quick decision when you really were not in a position to make the decision at all.

In addition to learning about the visitor's specific role in the process, your boothers can also learn about how decisions are made. This could include such things as vendor approvals or buying committees.

Here are some sample questions that should reveal the information staff will need.

- "What is your role in the company?"
- "Who is responsible for making decisions about new products?"

- "How are your family nutrition decisions made?
- "Who is going to have greater use for this product, you or your spouse?

Edgar Dunn and Emma Hope will confirm that they have a role in the process. Louis Fatale, Zelda Post, and Moe Lassis might be a bit cagey, but if staff listen carefully, they will learn that these visitors are not part of the decision-making process.

Ally McMate is a decision influencer. With the right questions, she can become a conduit to those who actually make decisions.

Don't forget that all visitors—whether they are decision influencers or decision makers, or if they have no part in the decision-making process—must all be treated respectfully, professionally, and politely.

C = CAPABILITY

Boothers need to determine whether the visitor or his or her organization can help them achieve their exhibiting objectives. Not all decision makers are the same. The decision makers are Edgar Dunn and Emma Hope, but Edgar is the only real buyer because Emma is not ready. The "capability" questions are often more general in nature. What these questions create is a thumbnail sketch of the visitors and their organizations. It gives the boother information to ascertain whether a visitor fits the definition of the target customer (see Chapter 3). With a few simple, non-threatening questions, a pattern develops. Ask:

- "Tell me a bit about your company."
- "What do you do?"
- "How many employees do you have?"
- "Where do you work?"
- "How long have you been at this location?"
- "What products are you currently using to solve this problem?"

And for many, the most important question of all is "Do you have a budget set aside for this upgrade?"

Edgar Dunn, Emma Hope, and Ally McMate might reveal information that fits your company's profile of a target visitor.

Zelda Post may say something like, "I'm between jobs at the moment."

Moe Lassis will be vague at best.

The capability questions help bring the picture into focus, but stopping here can leave the boother wasting valuable time with people such as Moe Lassis, Zelda Post, or Louis Fatale.

T = TIME

Time at an exhibit is always limited and should be properly allocated in order to see hundreds of visitors. Boothers need to decide how much time to spend with each visitor. If visitors have the potential of using your product or service sometime within your sales cycle (Edgar Dunn or Ally McMate), they should be given more time than the visitor who might be interested some day (Emma Hope).

Spending excess time with a visitor who might have a need outside the company's sales cycle (Emma Hope) wastes valuable opportunities. A better approach with these people is to give them a bit of information and put their contact information into follow-up initiatives. Emma Hope may have long-term potential, but she is not ready now. The bottom line is for staff to spend booth time with the visitors who can help move them closer to meeting their objectives.

Time is also an issue after the exhibit closes. Good follow-up (see Chapter 15) is done in a timely manner. There are many demands on your staff's time after the show is over. When they return to the office, they will face a mountain of phone and e-mails messages and will also have many leads that require follow-up. The first thing to do is prioritize these leads. Use time as the criteria as to who goes to the top of the priority list. If they get sidetracked by money or nice people or decision makers, they can miss opportunities. The focus should be on visitors who need attention quickly. This does not mean ignoring the rest. The time criterion is what determines the priority for follow-up.

The questions that differentiate Edgar Dunn from Emma Hope are:

- "When do you want to proceed with this idea?"
- "How soon should I contact you to set up an appointment?"
- "When are you thinking of going ahead with this initiative?"
- "When is the next open to buy?"

If a boother is dealing with Ally McMate, he or she might influence the timing by saying, "I am sure your boss will want to take advantage of this great offer. Would you please let her know that our show special expires on January 15th?"

I = IDENTITY

Knowing the visitor's name is an important part of the rapport process. Finding out a visitor's name is easy—read the visitor's show badge, exchange business cards, or simply say, "Hi, my name is Barry Siskind. I represent the ABC Company, and you are ... ?" But building rapport is much more than addressing a visitor by name.

Here is an example of a poor post-show follow-up phone call.

"Hi, Mr. Dunn, it's Bob Smith calling. We met at the Builder's Show last week and you expressed interest in our new line of shingles."

"Yes," Edgar Dunn answers. He is actually relieved that Bob Smith has followed up so quickly as he was really interested in the new line of shingles. "I'm glad you called."

"The purpose of the call," Bob continues, "is to set up a time for the two of us to get together to discuss your needs in more detail. I know you were really interested in our new line at the show."

"Great," Edgar responds, "How about early next week?"

So far so good. Now here is where the conversation falls apart.

"Sure," Bob says, "Mr. Dunn, before we confirm a time, let me ask you a couple of questions."

"Fire away."

"Okay. How are decisions like this made in your organization? Tell me a bit about your company. Do you have a budget? Do you ... "

"Hold on," Edgar says irritably. "Didn't you ask me all that when we met?"

"Yes, sir, I suppose I did," Bob answers sheepishly.

"Then why are you asking me again?"

"I guess I forgot." And there go all those nice feelings out the window.

Taking notes is often left to chance, perhaps on the back of a business card, scraps of paper, or a notebook. Boothers are left with inconsistent information from lead to lead. What they manage to jot down is what they remember.

Taking notes on the back of a business card is the worst of the lot. Some cultures view their cards as an extension of themselves and defacing the card in any way is a no-no.

Relying on business cards also presents additional problems. Some people print both sides of their cards, leaving little room for notes, and others use color paper or synthetic materials that eliminate the possibility of taking notes. The space on the back of a card is small, limiting the amount of information that can be recorded.

Let's look at some more effective information-gathering techniques.

The real benefit of exhibiting is not in the compliments you receive for your great-looking booth or the good times your staff had while out of town on a company credit card. The real rewards are tied into the information that you and your staff bring back that will result in ongoing business opportunities.

Information gathering in an environment where there is not much time for more than crowd control is a real challenge. One of the tools available to help exhibitors is a lead-retrieval system.

Anyone who has visited a trade show has probably seen exhibitors using one of the twelve to fifteen different versions of a lead-retrieval system. These systems might utilize a bar code reader, a scanner, or simply a device to swipe a plastic identification card. Some systems are available with dedicated hardware, while some can be add-ons to your personal computing devices. Whatever the system, anything that enables an exhibitor to gather quality information quickly is worth looking into.

Lead-retrieval systems are arranged for by show management. There is only one system available to rent at each show, although some exhibitors go to the expense of creating something that works specifically for them. The system is tied into the entire registration process. As each delegate registers, the information he or she records is entered into a database. The system then gives exhibitors access to some of this information. However, not all systems are created equally. Before you sign up, here are a few questions that need to be clarified.

What Information Does the System Provide?

There are certain basic bits of information beyond a name and address that exhibitors will find helpful. These could include: decision-making ability, budget, timing of the purchase, previous experience with the product or your company, obstacles to advancing the conversation to the next step of the sales cycle, and whether there is a need for the product or service. The more information you and your staff have, the better you will be able to conduct an effective post-show follow-up. The system being offered may provide all or some of the information you need.

In What Form Will I Receive the Information?

Manual systems in which the exhibitor swipes an identification card provide only the information encoded on the card. Additional information needs to be added manually by the exhibitor while qualifying the prospect. Other systems print out a hard copy of the information through the system vendor's computer or is stored in an electronic file. Knowing the form of the information enables you and your staff to plan properly.

When Will I Get the Information?

With a card-swipe device, you get the information immediately. For other systems there might be a twenty-four-hour turn around. Pay particular attention to how fast you will receive the information collected on the last day.

What Is the Cost?

Generally access to the system is not cost prohibitive. Scanners and readers can be rented for a few hundred dollars, but it's always best to check first.

What Information Does the System Not Give Me?

In some cases the system might have a printout that allows you to record additional information. But if you need more, then the solution is to create a manual lead card to use in conjunction with the system. This will save time in gathering the repetitive information already in the system and the manual card will provide what is missing in the printout. After the show, it is now a simple job to combine these two documents.

Is My Staff Comfortable with the System?

Often show management or the system provider will provide special training to help exhibitors become familiar with the system. Find out if this is available and take advantage of the opportunity. If your staff are not comfortable with the technology, they will not use the system to its advantage.

Information gathering is more than returning from the show with a pile of business cards for follow-up. Lead-retrieval systems can fill the gap. If the show or event you are participating in does not have a formal system or the system provided does not do the job, consider a lead card to ensure that information is collected properly.

Lead Cards

Lead cards are a formalized manual method of recording lead information for post-show follow-up. While the benefits of lead-retrieval systems are great, one must avoid the temptation of relying on them to give you all the information you need. Some do and some don't. Use a lead card either on its own or in concert with the lead-retrieval system. Here are some tips to help you create a lead card for your next show.

1. Your lead card is a pre-printed form that includes all the information staff will need to qualify their prospects, such as

decision-making ability, budgets, time frame, needs, etc. It should also have additional room to record anecdotal information, personal preferences, and any promises a staff person makes.

If you use your lead card in conjunction with the lead-retrieval system, then knowing what the system *doesn't* give is the clue to what questions you should include on your lead card. Most systems will provide basic demographic information, but do not take into account personal preferences, any problems the prospect has had in the past, or specific solutions the prospect is looking for.

2. A perfect size for this card is 4" × 7" (10 cm × 18 cm), which fits comfortably in a jacket, blazer, or pants pocket. It should also be small enough not to be mistaken as an order form or application of some sort.

3. Your lead card can be in pads of fifteen to twenty sheets. Keep the thickness of your lead card pads to a minimum to avoid tearing when inserted and removed from pockets. Pads also come with a cardboard backing, which provides a hard surface to write on.

4. Another trick is to create your lead cards as a duplicate form. This is really handy for exhibitors who want to give one copy to the sales rep for immediate follow-up and the second copy to sales or marketing management for future use.

5. Don't wait until the presentation is over and the visitor has left to complete the lead card. It is appropriate for staff to record their conversations while talking with visitors..

    If staff feel uncomfortable about writing notes in front of a visitor, they should think of recording this information as a nonverbal way of emphasizing the importance of the information. Staff can ask visitors, "Do you mind if I jot down some of this information?"

6. One more tip for your lead card is to add a section for follow-up. Your visitors will appreciate receiving follow-up information in a method that best suits them, so ask, "What is the best method for me to stay in touch with you?" Also add, "Do you mind if I keep you on our follow-up list?" This confirmation is needed to comply with any privacy concerns. Their recorded response enables you to construct your follow-up planning.

LEAD CARD
International Training &
Management Company
www.siskindtraining.com

Date: _____

Authority: _____

Capability: _____

Time: _____

Identity: _____

    Name: _____

    Position: _____

    Organization: _____

    Address: _____

    Telephone: _____

Obstacles: _____

Need: _____

_____

Promised Follow-Up: _____

_____

Comments: _____

_____

_____

Do we have your permission to contact you in the future?
☐ Yes ☐ No

© ITMC-2005

Whether booth staff's purpose during a show is taking orders, selling products from your booth, creating awareness of your company or product, or looking for people they can do business with after the show, lead cards are the most important tool.

Good boothers should get into the habit of completing a lead card for every visitor except Zelda Post, Louis Fatale, and Moe Lassis—there really is no point in taking the time.

Whether you use a manual lead card, a lead-retrieval system, or combine the two, a crucial part of exhibiting success is based on the information these tools give you. Use them wisely.

O = OBSTACLES

Boothers have created a snapshot of visitors' situations by determining the decision-making process and the urgency for a solution, and they have begun recording all the information. What could possibly be missing?

A common trap for many boothers is when a visitor sounds very much like Edgar Dunn, but in reality he is a cleverly disguised Louis Fatale. A common dilemma for exhibitors is spending lots of time with a visitor, only to find out later that there is an obstacle in doing business. There are always reasons why visitors cannot or will not do business.

Some of these reasons include loyalties to a competitor, existing contractual arrangements, past history with your company, location outside your service area, vendor restrictions, or technical incompatibility. Every visitor can create his or her own special list of obstacles. The trick is to uncover these obstacles as quickly as possible. If the obstacle takes time to deal with or cannot be overcome, boothers may choose to deal with the visitor at a later date or simply move to the disengagement.

All six players can throw obstacles in the path. Boothers must listen carefully to what visitors say and carefully decide how to proceed. One common mistake is letting the obstacle derail the qualifying effort.

Uncovering obstacles doesn't necessarily mean that the conversation is over and all is lost. In fact, a skillfully handled obstacle can open up new opportunities. When boothers discover the obstacle, they acknowledge it and continue with the job at hand—qualifying. The exception is when the obstacle makes it evident that the player, such as Zelda Post, Moe Lassis, or Louie Fatale, has little value.

Some questions that will reveal hidden obstacles are: "Have you conducted business with our company in the past?" or "If our product fits your requirements, is there any reason we can't do business?"

Obstacle questions will quickly reveal problems and are a good way to get Moe Lassis to reveal his true identity.

One final word about obstacles. Often boothers are reluctant to ask a question that may invoke a negative response. Why topple the apple cart? The answer is simple. If there is some reason that this prospect cannot or will not do business, the prospect already knows it. By asking the obstacle question, your boothers create a level playing field where everything is on the table and decisions about proceeding can be made properly.

N = NEED

The order of the first five ACTION questions is irrelevant—be flexible. The need question, which falls at the end of the ACTION acronym, is really the first question a boother should ask. Previously you learned that 40 percent of visitors will avoid any commitment because they perceive that boothers don't understand their needs. Here is a chance to prove them wrong. The need question addresses their needs rather than the boother's.

Questions such as, "Can I show you our new widget?" or "Do you have a couple of minutes to take part in our demonstration?" all focus on your boother's need. A good need question puts the focus where it really should be—on the visitor.

The need question is a bridge from breaking the ice to gathering information and the ACTION process. Once boothers have broken the ice, they should follow up quickly with questions such as: "Tell me a bit about your situation now," or "What were you hoping to find at the show?" or "Do you use this technology now?"

Information gathering is not a lengthy process. In fact, once some proficiency in asking the right question is developed, the identity of the player will be revealed in the first minute or two of conversation. One final word about information gathering. What if the visitor doesn't want to take part in this carefully planned play? What if visitors interrupt the information gathering with questions of their own? It is so easy to get sidetracked. Remember, boothers need to maintain control and time is best controlled when they ask questions. However, if they ignore visitors' questions, they are perceived negatively. If the visitor interrupts and asks a question, a quick answer will suffice. For example:

> *Visitor*: "Does this also come in blue?"
>
> *Boother*: "Yes, as a matter of fact there are several shades of blue. Before I show you what's available, let me ask you a couple of questions so I can focus on the best solution for you."

Or

> *Visitor*: "Okay, you have thirty seconds to tell me all about your new product."
>
> *Boother*: "There is so much to tell that I don't know where to start. Let me ask you a couple of questions that will let me know what your interests are."

Gathering information is at the heart of the boother's job.

IN CONCLUSION

You are now at the half-way point of your four-act play. However, it's not time to take an intermission. You need the next step to keep the visitor interested. You must present some meaningful information.

Making Effective Show Presentations

"Do what you can, with what you have, where you are."
— Theodore Roosevelt —

The world's top chefs all know that the real secret of a successful dish is in its presentation. The same holds true for marketers, salespeople, and consultants. Balancing all the show logistics often means that the preparation of a good booth presentation gets left to chance. Often they are too long or too short, too comprehensive, or provide scarcely enough information for the visitor to make a decision.

Once the visitor has been qualified, boothers can decide how to best spend the next few minutes productively. Edgar Dunn, Emma Hope, and Ally McMate are qualified for information about products or services. Louis Fatale, Zelda Post, and Moe Lassis are not qualified, so boothers can skip this act and proceed immediately to the disengagement. This may sound cold and heartless, but at a show boothers have to be extremely careful about how they spend their time.

MAINTAIN FOCUS

Making presentations to people who have no use for the product or service is a waste of time. In the initial planning, an objective for the exhibit was established. This objective is the guide that keeps your staff focused throughout every stage of their show participation. Moreover, it will dictate the content of the booth presentation. Boothers have to be flexible. The best presentation is one that focuses on the visitor.

GOOD TIME MANAGEMENT PRACTICES

The key to an effective booth presentation is to remember that while a show is a great a place to capture a visitor's interest, it is generally not the best place for a detailed discussion. In most cases, this discussion is better left to the peace and quiet of a follow-up visit.

Because time is at a premium, the presentation should be only long enough to achieve the objective and whet the visitors' post-show appetite. Develop a presentation that your staff can use that will work within their time constraints. A presentation that attempts to tell the prospect the whole story is overdoing it. Including too much will add to the confusion that visitors may already be experiencing. A good presentation should take from one to seven minutes, depending on boothers' objectives. If the objective is to generate leads for post-exhibit follow-up, then the presentation can be shorter. If the objective is to obtain an order immediately, then the presentation might even exceed the seven-minute limit. One to seven minutes may not seem like much time, but a well-structured presentation can cover a lot of ground in a short time.

According to psychologists, the human brain can remember five pieces of information at one time. Tell visitors too much, and the chances that they will remember all of it are slim. It is better to introduce the key elements and leave them wanting more in a follow-up visit.

THE PRESENTATION

This third act in the play is a chance to leave a lasting impression. A canned presentation delivered by rote is inappropriate. The overriding principal in a presentation is: **Tell visitors what they *want* to know rather than *what* they need to know.** Staff should memorize and use this as a mantra to be repeated mentally before each presentation commences.

What visitors *want* to know comes from their perspective. These wants were uncovered during the information-gathering process.

What visitors *need* to know is from your boother's point of view. The visitor will ultimately need to know everything, but not now. In most situations, if the visitor leaves your exhibit remembering that the boother has a viable solution, that's the best that can be hoped for.

Prior to the show you created an analysis of the potential audience. This will help your boothers to focus on the individual needs of their visitors rather than looking at everyone as one homogeneous group.

Visitor Type

The first step is to analyze the show visitors. In Chapter 3 we discussed features and benefits, now it's time to take this discussion one step further. The show or event manager may be of some help here. He or she can often provide details of the attendee population at past events. This list can be limited to the six players or you might expand this list to include such people as the media, different types of immediate buyers, industry consultants, students, public or private sector visitors, and so on. Be as detailed as possible to help your boothers know who they will be dealing with.

List the concerns that each type of visitor might have. This is a great eye-opener. When you examine the visitor's concerns from his or her perspective, it can shed a new light on the potential for your exhibit. It will also allow your boothers to fully understand the challenges they face and must prepare for. Some visitor types are identical, while others may have special differences. For example, owners and consultants have a similar interest and can be grouped in one category. Purchasing agents and the media are different and warrant separate consideration.

Identify the proof statements you have to back up each of your claims. Proof statements are specific pieces of evidence to support your claims. Proof statements can be derived from testimonials, lists of client users, articles in trade magazines, consumer reports, product specification sheets, and so on. Proof statements during a demonstration are generic. Proof statements in the presentation phase arespecific. A boother might back up a claim to a visitor by saying, "This is our most popular model. As a matter of fact, six out of ten people in your position have already seen the advantages of using it." The visitor may say, "That's good to know," in which case your boother can move on to the next benefit. Alternatively the visitor may respond with, "Many people in my business don't understand the new technology." In this case the visitor has just taken the wind out of your proof statement. Your boothers will need additional sources they can use if one doesn't work. When you generate a list of proof statements, your boothers can choose the one they think will work best with each visitor they are presenting to. If the boother guessed wrong, he or she will have more as a backup.

Your analysis might look something like the following:

EVENT NAME: THE NATIONAL GARDEN SHOW		
Visitor Type	*Concerns*	*Proof*
Gardening enthusiasts	• New products • Best practices • Soil and nutrition advice	• Trade magazine articles • Examples from experts • Manufacturer specs
Spouse of gardening enthusiasts	• New products • Appropriate gift • Cost	• Trade magazine articles • User profile • Spec sheets
Retailers	• Innovative products • What's selling well • What people are asking for	• Samples • Sales results • Anecdotal evidence
Media	• Innovative products • Success stories • Environmental issues	• Samples • Sales results • Manufacturers' specs or warnings

This is a terrific pre-event exercise to do with all your staff. Often during the brainstorming process, great insights are generated that you might have ignored if you had completed this pre-event analysis on your own. The other advantage of creating this analysis in a group is that it helps your entire booth staff realize the number of different perspectives they will be dealing with, and it gets your boothers involved in the show plans early.

One final word. This pre-event analysis is based on assumptions. When boothers gather information, they need to listen carefully to verify the assumptions. Just because they assumed that one type of visitor was interested in three things does not mean that is true. Gardening enthusiasts, for example, may be interested in soil and nutrition advice, so telling them about new products or show specials is a waste of time.

This pre-event analysis provides your boothers with a platform to begin the development of a good exhibit presentation.

Preparing the Presentation

Remember this old newspaper formula: "Tell them what you are going to tell them, tell them, and tell them what you have just told them"? It's the key function of the three parts to an effective presentation—the opening, the body, and the close.

All three parts are needed because as great as your product or service might be, the visitor has already been inundated with information. A methodical approach gives visitors time to absorb what they are hearing. Your boothers are providing a letter-perfect picture that the visitor will have trouble ignoring.

The Opening: Tell Them What You Are Going to Tell Them

The opening is a graceful bridge from information gathering to information giving. It focuses the visitor's attention on how your product or service can meet his or her needs. This bridge is important because boothers need to keep prospects moving along with them. The bridge could be as simple as "Let me take a moment to show you how our widget will help you accomplish the economies you are looking for."

During the information-gathering phase, the boother will have established the visitor's wants, so restate them. The more boothers can organize visitors' thoughts, the better. Visitors suffer from *information overload*. Don't add to the overload. Recognize it and help visitors put information into neat little packages. For Edgar Dunn, a boother can say, "I would also like to show you how our widget will take care of your other concerns, which are product compatibility and ongoing maintenance."

For Emma Hope, a boother can try, "Let me tell you a few things to keep in mind when the time is right."

For Ally McMate a boother might say, "Here are a couple of key points your colleagues will appreciate knowing about."

For Louis Fatale, Zelda Post, and Moe Lassis, your boother should have already decided that a presentation is not necessary and moved on to the disengagement.

The last part of the opening is to let the visitor know the next steps. This ensures that there is a level playing field and that there will be no misunderstandings or surprises. A statement such as "I hope that once you see a few of the advantages of our widgets, we will be able to get together after the show for a more detailed presentation," will keep the boother and visitor on the same track.

The visitor and the boother know what the presentation will cover. The two or three key points should form the outline for the body of the presentation.

The Body: Tell Them

The body of the presentation is made up of the individual concerns that your product or service can solve for a particular visitor. Deal with one concern at a time because it's easier for your visitor to stay focused. The visitor doesn't have the advantage of an instant replay. If the visitor misses something, he or she may or may not ask, but one thing at a time is the best bet.

What your visitor wants is something that will solve a problem. There is an old saying in sales training: "People buy solutions." Most visitors you speak to at a show are looking for specific solutions to problems. Once you understand these problems, the next step is to address them. Not all transactions are simple. Your boother may have to describe your product or service or proposal. The boother may have to convey background information to help the visitor make choices, and this is where many boothers run into trouble—they fail to communicate solutions effectively.

The average boother talks about the product or service in terms of features—the product or service's actual physical characteristics. Talking in terms of benefits, however, can go a long way toward improving the communication link between boother and visitor because when boothers talk about benefits, they tell visitors what the product or service will do for them.

Each concern then is dealt with by stating the feature, first followed quickly by the benefit (what the feature will do for the prospect). Then the benefit is followed by a quick proof statement. It goes something like this: "Our kryptonite-based (feature) widget will help you achieve the economies you are looking for (benefit). We have had considerable success with other manufacturers in your industry and have been able to show them as much as a 53 percent decrease in costs (proof)."

Then the boother should confirm that he or she has made the point by asking the prospect, "How does that sound?" Looking for reinforcement and asking questions keeps the visitor involved and ensures that the proofs were meaningful.

If the visitor agrees, bridge to the next area of their concern with a simple statement such as, "Now let me deal with the compatibility issue." If they don't agree, introduce a second proof statement and check back to see if it had more impact.

By handling one concern at a time, the visitor will be less likely to be overwhelmed by details. If the presentation is well received, a post-show meeting can be arranged with the appropriate amount of time needed to review all of the features and benefits.

The Close: Tell Them What You Have Just Told Them

If handled properly, the closing sets up a number of important steps. It confirms that the visitor is interested, it sets the tone for follow-up activities, and it helps the boother disengage.

The close starts with a quick review of the visitor's concerns and the features and benefits of your products or services. The proofs are not necessary. Repetition is a key learning principle, so don't worry about the visitor objecting. In fact, it will probably be quite the opposite. The summary puts the whole discussion into a nice package and makes it easy for the visitor to make a decision. For example, "I've shown you how our new widget effectively handles the problem of compatibility and we have discussed the requirements for ongoing maintenance."

The next step is to ask for a commitment. Lots of business is lost because a commitment was not requested. Some boothers feel uncomfortable with this step because there is a perception that by asking, things will change. The boother and visitor have been having a nice chat, so why push it? When your boothers use this presentation structure, asking for the commitment is the logical next step. Asking is not a surprise because the visitor was forewarned. In the first part of the presentation, the visitor understood where the presentation was going. By ignoring this next step, the boother is leaving the visitor uncertain about what he or she should do next. The solution is to be proactive—ask for the commitment.

Asking for a commitment is a great way to ease into an effective disengagement with the visitor. Here is an example: "The next step is for us to schedule a time to get together to examine the whole picture. When would be a good time to do that?" Or "I would like to pass your information along to one of our area representatives who will call to schedule an appointment to take you through the next steps."

The final move is leaving the visitor with a positive feeling about the relationship that has been initiated: "I am looking forward to meeting you on the 15th." Your boother is now ready for the disengagement.

An effective show presentation is the heart of the sales interaction. Good planning, effective time management, and flexibility will make the presentation direct, meaningful, and, most of all, profitable.

IN CONCLUSION

You have successfully broken the ice, gathered information, and made an effective show presentation. You have peaqued the visitors interest, arranged for some follow-up activity, or taken the order. Now what? The visitor doesn't seem to want to leave. This is why the last act of our play is crucial.

Disengaging

---

*"The door of opportunity won't open
unless you do some pushing."*
— Anonymous —

Imagine this: You have just had an engaging conversation with a visitor. You approached, gathered important information about the visitor's business needs, felt some rapport, suggested solutions, gave the visitor crucial information that he or she responded positively to, and received a commitment to a follow-up meeting. Sounds pretty good, right? But there is one more challenge. The visitor doesn't seem to want to leave.

The last step is to wrap up the conversation effectively and move on to the next visitor. On the show floor, effective time management is a boother's most valuable asset. There is nothing wrong with spending extra time with a visitor and getting into a detailed discussion during low-traffic times.

However, at high-traffic periods, important opportunities will be missed. Disengaging is neither rude nor impolite. When handled properly, it leaves the visitor with a positive feeling about the boother, the company, and its products or services. The trick is to stay focused on objectives and develop the skill to end the conversation gracefully.

Disengaging can be easy. It is the logical end of a presentation— the boother agrees on a follow-up, thanks the visitor for his or her time with a handshake, and moves on: "Mr. Smith, it has been great meeting you today. I'll get that information out to you as soon as I return to my office and then I'll call to set up an appointment. Thanks for your interest and enjoy the rest of the show."

But sometimes disengaging can present a real challenge—some visitors will chat all day if you let them. Time will be squandered if the conversation continues needlessly. The show is a place of business and once the business of the day is complete, it is time to move on.

With some planning, boothers can avoid the disengagement trap. There are two types of disengaging strategies: the presumptive disengagement and the conciliatory disengagement.

THE PRESUMPTIVE DISENGAGEMENT

If you have planned your exhibit properly, your boothers will have plenty of tools to use with this technique. Some of these tools are promotional products; literature; in-booth activities such as demonstrations, seminars, draws; or when all else fails, a business card. The trick is to call on the right tool at the right time.

This technique simply presumes that the boother and visitor are in agreement, the business at hand has been concluded, and it's time to move on. There are three parts to the presumptive disengagement technique: refocus, the setup, and the proposition.

Step 1: Refocus

The first step of the process is to refocus the visitor's attention. Up until now the focus has been on business. Time was spent reviewing the visitor's situation and information was presented that let the visitor know how your product or service can satisfy his or her needs. If the objective was to write an order, this has now been completed and the visitor is happy. If the objective was to generate the lead, that has now been accomplished. If there was a communication objective, then the relevant information has been passed along. The boother needs to refocus the visitor's attention and gracefully end the conversation. The refocus stage is a subtle way of saying, "I am drawing this conversation to its conclusion." This is accomplished when the boother stops presenting and says, "I am pleased that we had a chance to take a look at your situation," or "I'm glad that we had an opportunity to talk today," or "I am looking forward to getting your feedback once you have received your initial order."

Step 2: The Setup

This is an important step of the process as it clearly makes the point. The boother takes full responsibility for the disengagement by saying, "I know you are anxious to see the rest of the show," or "I've already taken enough of your time."

Step 3: The Proposition

Studies have shown that a visitor who leaves a booth with something tangible to show for the visit has a stronger feeling about that company or the visit than when leaving a booth empty-handed. Using promotional products or brochures as an approach tool robs your boothers of an excellent disengagement opportunity.

Offering visitors something at the end of the conversation is a better use of these tools. This allows boothers to thank the visitor for stopping by and gives the offering real value. Boothers might say, "We have created this new promotional gift for some of our special booth visitors. You can see our web site has been engraved on the side, so if you want to learn more about what we do, please visit us on-line. Thanks for spending time at our booth." Or "We have a demonstration starting in less than one minute that will give you some additional information. If you have the time, let me get you a seat right up front." Or "This brochure has the information you asked about. The information on page nine gets into the more technical side of our new product. I will follow up with you next week. Thanks for dropping by and enjoy the rest of the show."

If Louis Fatale stops by and asks lots of questions, but there is little chance of doing any real business, say, "Here is my business card. If you have any further questions, please don't hesitate to visit our web site or give me a call." The chance of him actually calling is remote. Don't waste valuable promotional products, literature, or a seat at the demonstration.

THE CONCILIATORY DISENGAGEMENT

Conversations that do not lead toward achieving show objectives need to be derailed quickly. These can include existing customers who want to chat, but are not interested in purchasing additional products at this time; other exhibitors who want to monopolize your time because they are bored; people who are selling their products or services to exhibitors; or students who were invited by show management.

The solution is the conciliatory approach. Boothers need to be vigilant. Louis Fatale, Edgar Dunn, Emma Hope, Ally McMate, Zelda Post, and Moe Lassis are charming people who engage boothers in a conversation. When the show is slow, boothers tend to want to talk to all of these people. They are nice, they help pass the time, and boothers have nothing better to do. The problem is that once boothers are engaged in one conversation, they will ignore other potential visitors as they walk by. They should assess each visitor and spend show time with the right people—the visitors who can help achieve show objectives.

Maintaining control over the conversation and asking qualifying questions early in the dialogue will reveal the visitor's agenda quickly.

There are four steps to the conciliatory disengagement: the acknowledgment, the invitation, the reality check, and the call to action.

Step 1: The Acknowledgment

The last thing boothers want to do is to appear rude, unfriendly, or unprofessional. They never want to leave anyone, regardless of their ability to do business, with a negative impression. Boothers work in a fishbowl and are under the scrutiny of every passer-by. Other visitors will see how your boothers treat people, and a negative attitude may affect their willingness to approach.

If the visitor cannot help a boother achieve current show objectives, the boother should move to disengage by acknowledging the visitor as follows:

- *For an established customer who is not buying anything more at this time*: "Thanks for dropping by this afternoon. I am really pleased to know that we can count on your ongoing business."
- *To a fellow exhibitor*: "Thanks for dropping by. It's important that we keep each other in our networks. You never know when an opportunity may come up when we need to speak."
- *To a student*: "I am glad that you have chosen our company as the focus of your research."
- *To a vendor*: "There is always the possibility that your product is something we can use in the future."

Step 2: The Invitation

Boothers never know when opportunity will knock. They need to be open to surprises. When they cut a visitor off too soon, valuable insight that could prove beneficial in the future may be lost. Step 2, the invitation, forces boothers to maintain this awareness:

- *To an existing customer*: "I really need to hear your feedback. It helps me and my company grow and ensures that we meet your needs."
- *To an exhibitor*: "I would like to find out more about your company and how it serves this industry."
- *To a student*: "Both my company and I believe in ensuring the continuity of our industry."
- *To a vendor*: "It might make sense for me to know a bit more about your product."

Step 3: Reality Check

This step is at the heart of the conciliatory disengagement. It is a simple explanation of the situation. Often the visitor doesn't realize that continuing the conversation at the booth is detrimental. A simple explanation sets the record straight. In this case say: "We have a challenge. Show management tells me that during the next few hours we can expect over 1,500 people. The best you and I can do is start a conversation that will be filled with interruptions."

Step 4: The Call to Action

The last phase of this technique is to set up a plan for the future. It's also a good way to test the visitor's seriousness. Here are some offers that can be made:

- *For the customer*: "This show is over on Wednesday and I am planning to visit your city early next week. Why don't we set up a time to get together and over coffee I can get all your feedback?" or "I am taking a break at 2:00 P.M. Could you meet me at the hospitality area where we can sit quietly and talk?"
- *To the exhibitor*: "My focus for this show is on the visitors and if someone drops by my booth, I will have to stop our conversation in mid-sentence to greet them. Why don't we meet for a drink after the show closes?"
- *To the student*: "You have come at a busy time. After 5:00 P.M. things will quiet down significantly. Why not drop by then?"
- *To the vendor*: "I really can't take time away from my focus. Why don't you give me a call next week when we can spend a few uninterrupted minutes exploring the potential of your product?"

IN CONCLUSION

The presumptive and conciliatory techniques will allow boothers to disengage 99 percent of the time. There may be the odd time when these do not work. When this happens, your booth staff need to develop strategies to help each other out, such as sending subtle signs for help or summoning a manager who can handle the really tough questions.

Disengaging doesn't come naturally; it requires practice. By not doing so when the time is right, your boothers will be underutilizing the show's possibilities.

Developing Rapport with Potential Clients

"The most important single ingredient
in the formula of success
is knowing how to get along with people"
— Theodore Roosevelt —

Stage 3 boothers have now mastered the skills of breaking the ice, gathering information, making the presentation, and disengaging. The next step is to make the transition from stage 3 to stage 4. Here boothers integrate the rapport process that enables them to connect with the visitor on a real and human level. At stage 4, boothers are not just asking questions to gain information, they are building a business relationship. The real question is how do your boothers position themselves so that more visitors will respond positively? Notice how I used the words "more visitors" rather than "all the visitors." This is the reality we all must face since, in spite of best efforts, boothers can't be everything to everybody. However, with a little understanding of how rapport is built, boothers will drastically improve their odds and extend their reach.

Think back to the people you feel comfortable with. It could be your spouse, other members of your family, colleagues, business associates, customers, the mailman. What is it about them that makes you feel comfortable?

It may have been a common experience you have with a particular situation—a movie you both appreciated, mutual friends and acquaintances, or a similar outlook on life. If you think back even further to the first time you met this person, you will discover there was something there from the first moment. Granted, we all have stories about people we found unpleasant at first and then, over time, learned to like, but in most situations, there is some spark present from the first moment. Take a walk to your favorite mall or restaurant and look at the strangers. Are there some strangers you feel different toward than others?

I have done this exercise many times. Often I find myself in malls doing book signings, where I will be sitting at a table in the front of a bookstore, waiting for people to come by. Fortunately, sometimes there are lots of people, but, as luck would have it, sometimes I just sit there and watch. Each person in the mall has a story to tell. He or she tells it nonverbally—through body movements; the way the person responds to another adult or child; how he or she regards salespeople in a store; how the person licks an ice cream cone. Sometimes I find myself staring at one person who has really caught my attention, and at other times my eyes quickly jump from one person to the next.

The process of rapport building begins long before introductions are made. We watch, we collect and process data, and we judge. There may be some strangers who simply walk by and avoid eye contact, hoping you don't see them. On the other hand, other strangers may smile, stop, and talk. When your boothers stand in the exhibit, everyone who passes by is doing the same thing that you and I do to strangers in the mall. Perhaps a smile, a nod of the head, or an interested look may go a long way, but rapport is so much more than that.

In the 1960s, psychologist Albert Mehrabrian conducted a groundbreaking experiment. He found that people judge other people based on three observable clues: words, the para-verbal, and the nonverbal.

WORDS

Words are what most of us use first when we analyze our reactions to people. Think about someone you met for the first time. You probably thought to your self, "What an interesting person. I really liked the way he answered that question. He is so articulate. That is exactly what I would have said." Or you may have thought, "This person is a real jerk." Either reaction was based on what the person said—the words—but words are only one part of the equation.

PARA-VERBAL

Para-verbal is not what you say but *how* you say it. It is the tone, pace, tempo, speed, or volume of your voice. We all listen to people and create impressions of them based on how they use their voices. This phenomena in most apparent when you eliminate the effects of their nonverbal behavior. Think about a time when you dealt with someone only on the telephone or through e-mail. You listened to the person's voice on the phone or read his or her correspondence. We often talk about the tone or pace of written correspondence. Now, after a lengthy relationship either on the phone or by e-mail, you have a chance to meet this person face to face. What are the chances that the person will look the way you think he or she will look? Pretty slim. Another good example of the power of para-verbal is when you listen to personalities on the radio. Day after day you drive to the office, listening to the host of the morning show, the newscaster, the weather man, and the traffic guy. They become familiar to you. Now suppose you met some of these people at a trade show or a special event. It's amazing how your impression of these people will change. We listen to how they use their voices and create a mental picture. There is one more element.

NONVERBAL

We are all guilty of judging people by what we see. It goes beyond the obvious color or racial differences that we rightfully try to avoid using to judge others. Nonverbal includes the entire physical package. Yes, we do judge a book by its cover. We might say, "There is a successful person—she has that look of confidence in her eyes," or "He's a loser—look at the way he is dressed."

What do para-verbal and nonverbal clues have to do with your work at an exhibition? Mehrabrian discovered that the relative importance of each in the equation is as follows:

> Words: 7 percent
> Para-verbal: 38 percent
> Nonverbal: 55 percent

When you combine the para-verbal and nonverbal, you realize that 93 percent of people's impressions of others are not directly related to *what* they say but *how* they say it—an important lesson for anyone in business.

Rather than telling visitors how much their business means to them, boothers should show them. Boothers who need to give highly technical information often say that the actual words are more important than the person saying them. While there may be some truth to this argument, if you don't trust the person you are talking to, it doesn't matter how intelligent he or she is. Their words will be interpreted skeptically.

Mehrabrian's study is valid in all human interactions. Build rapport with actions rather than words and rapport will develop faster and last longer.

PRIOR TO APPROACHING

When visitors walk by your exhibit, they form opinions based on what they see. If they like what they see, then the chances are greater that they will welcome an approach. If they don't. ...

Your boothers are on the front line. They are the first contact for the visitor and consequently set the pace for all future interactions. The visitor's opinion of the boother is also his or her opinion of your entire organization. Look at a number of do's and don'ts and see how boothers can influence visitors' opinions.

Don't #1: Sit

Working a show is a long and tiring job. Having chairs in your exhibit when there is no need for them will encourage booth staff to sit. Yes, it is a long day. Yes, their feet and back hurt, but sitting creates the impression that they are tired and that it is an effort to get up and take care of visitors. Visitors don't want to impose—so they don't.

If boothers have real physical problems with standing all day, then an option is a high stool strategically placed so they can rest on it rather than relax in it.

Don't #2: Eat or Drink

If boothers are sampling food products, they should remember that the samples are for the visitors. Exhibitors should also not run to the snack bar, grab a sandwich, and bring it back to the booth. The problem is perception. Visitors who walk past the booth and see boothers eating their lunch may feel that disturbing them will be an imposition—so they won't.

Coffee, tea, beer, and wine are all no-no's. The only exception to the rule is water. In fact, boothers should have a bottle of water kept in an inconspicuous place so they can sip on it during their booth duty. Water will refresh them and keep their throats lubricated. Caffeine, on the other hand, is a diuretic and will cause dryness, which is a leading cause of the hoarse throat that many boothers experience after a long day at an exhibition.

Don't #3: Talk to Colleagues

This is a symptom of the stage 1 boother. It's commonly referred to as the "exhibitor huddle" when two or more boothers are huddled together, deeply engaged in conversation, or when two or more boothers are congregated around one visitor. The result is a look that is less than inviting. Visitors walk by instead of interrupting the conversation. The result is lost opportunity.

Don't #4: Avoid Distractions

When boothers are busy, it's easy to stay focused. When things get slow, the mind wanders. There are many possible distractions, including newspapers, novels, office paperwork, brochures, other exhibitors, cell phones, interesting people, etc. Your boothers' attention must be focused on the job at hand 100 percent of the time.

Don't #5: Exercise

Deep knee bends, back stretches, and over-the-shoulder arm extensions relieve the stress, but from the visitors' point of view, sore feet or a stiff back are not of interest. Visitors should feel that the boothers are there for them 100 percent. Think about the people you do business with. Do you feel they are doing you a favor by showing up, or do they seem genuinely interested in their work and their commitment to fulfill promises? A message is planted in visitors' minds when they walk by your exhibit and see your boothers discreetly take off one shoe or flex their feet to give their legs a good stretch.

Do #1: Be Well Groomed

As 55 percent of visitors' impressions come from what they see, boothers need to create an impression that is consistent with the image they are trying to convey. The clothes they wear are an important part of the package. My recommendation is to take the exhibit seriously and dress in business attire—that is what would be worn when meeting with clients. Another option is theme clothing, such as t-shirts or sweatshirts. The advantages of theme clothing are the following:

1. It is easy for visitors to find help.

2. Clothes can tie into the colors and messaging found elsewhere in the exhibit.

3. It takes the burden off each boother to know what is appropriate attire and what is not.

4. There is ongoing promotion for the exhibit whenever your boother walks around the show or event.

The only disadvantage is that when your entire booth staff are dressed the same way, mistakes are magnified. The "exhibitor huddle" now looks like a sports team preparing for the next move.

Here are some tips to consider when choosing theme clothing:

1. *Choose something that is gender neutral*: There are many choices of clothing that convey a "unisex" image and are appropriate for everyone.

2. *Choose clothing that will suit all body shapes*: Your staff come in all shapes and sizes and you don't want people to feel uncomfortable in a particular garment.

3. *Provide a change*: If your show or event will last longer than one day, you want your staff to look fresh each day. Either provide enough clothing to last them through the whole show or arrange for an overnight cleaning service.

4. *Select good-quality clothing*: Ensure that your choice is of good quality. Your image is at stake and tears, holes, lint balls, or hanging threads will project an unfavorable impression.

5. *Make theme clothing mandatory*: Once you have chosen to use theme clothing, it must be mandatory for all booth staff. If some choose not to wear it and others do, it lessens the impact of the clothing and your overall booth.

6. *Be open to options*: Theme clothing can include jackets, ties, armbands, hats, jewelry, scarves, or suits. Be open in your thinking and find theme clothing that reflects the image and marketing message you want to convey.

Do #2: Know (and Like) Your Products

Many boothers are concerned about not being able to answer every question. Having full knowledge about every product or service isn't realistic. The larger the organization, the less likely it is that each boother will have a firm grasp on everything. The need to have answers for everything is a self-imposed trap. Visitors expect a reasonable amount of knowledge from the people they deal with and they also expect (and deserve) honest answers. If a boother doesn't have an answer, it's okay. The boother should not fake it. The visitor will understand as long as the boother makes every effort to find the answer or steers the visitor in the right direction.

It's up to you, the exhibit manager, to provide the information that boothers need to handle tough questions. This can take the form of having a 1-800 number that visitors can call, information on the web site, technical people at the booth, a customer service hot line, etc. Rather than expecting your boothers to have complete product knowledge, it's more important that they love your product or service. If they are really convinced that what they represent will be of benefit to those who eventually use it and if they like the organization they represent, then encourage them to bring this passion with them to the show. Their genuine enthusiasm is a much greater asset than being expected to know everything.

Do #3: Act Professionally

In the marketing mix there are many tools available. One of the advantages of exhibiting is that your staff will meet many targeted people in a short period. This is face-to-face marketing at its very best. The bottom line is that boothers should take their time at an exhibit seriously. A visitor's first impression is made in a millisecond. It may take forever to correct a negative impression.

RAPPORT DURING THE ICE BREAKER

When a boother first greets the visitor, it's difficult to know how this person will react. If a timid visitor is greeted by a loud and boisterous "Hello!" there is a good chance this person will quickly move on to the next booth. With such a huge mismatch in communication styles, the differences can be startling and produce a response that is detrimental to the boother's objectives. The best way to approach visitors is in a manner that is most compatible with the way they normally act. The problem is that boothers don't know what that might be. When they have time, they can gather clues by watching visitors' nonverbal behavior. However, during the busiest times boothers won't have this luxury. They will disengage from one visitor and have another waiting.

Here are some of the key elements to incorporate into your boothers nonverbal and para-verbal behavior.

- *Enthusiasm*: Enthusiasm is contagious. When your boothers are passionate about and committed to the solutions your organization offers, their enthusiasm is conveyed to the visitors they meet.
- *Eye contact*: There are always cultural considerations, but most visitors respond well when boothers make and maintain direct eye contact during the conversation—that is, focus on the visitor and the situation.
- *Questions about needs*: Boothers should find out about the visitors' needs. Approaching and talking about themselves is presumptuous.
- *Handshaking*: Studies have shown that 83 percent of booth personnel will not shake an attendee's hand. If boothers want to stand out in the crowd, they should introduce themselves and greet visitors the same way they would at a reception, wedding, or any other social affair.
- *Smile*: If your boothers are happy to be there, they should show it. A smile goes a long way toward making visitors feel at ease. If your boothers' feet are aching and they feel overworked, they should hide their discomfort. Visitors do not feel comfortable thinking they are a burden.
- *Act the host*: The exhibit is like a home away from home. Let's pretend that you have recently moved into a new neighborhood. You decide to have an open house for the neighbors. You are all set up and look your best. When your guests arrive at your door, you take on the role of the host. You invite them in, make them comfortable,

and talk to them. This is the same attitude each boother should have at a show. It's their place of business and visitors have been invited. They should approach visitors like a host and make them feel welcome.

- *Observe*: From the instant the conversation begins, the boother is assessing the visitor. In the second act of the play, boothers are gathering specific information that will determine how they will spend their time with the visitor. In addition, boothers also need information that tells them how to act with this visitor in a comfortable and businesslike manner.

Rapport building starts the minute the conversation begins. Listen and watch how the visitor answers your boother's questions. Study the para-verbal and nonverbal.

Para-verbal clues will reveal that some people speak loudly and others are soft-spoken, some will talk fast and others slowly, some have lots of inflection in their voice and others are monotone.

Nonverbal clues reveal that some people are demonstrative and others are standoffish, some will stand tall with perfect posture and others will slouch, some will come inside your personal space and others will keep their distance.

While many of the differences may be cultural, they all give strong clues on how booth staff should proceed. They need to read the clues properly and take the first important step toward building rapport. If they ignore the clues, a wall will develop between the boother and the visitor.

Let's assume a prospect approached and your boother asks a well thought-out question. Let's suppose that the visitor replies in a soft voice. If your boother is normally a loud person and does not adjust his or her voice to accommodate, the boother will alienate the visitor. If visitors feel uncomfortable, a wall of indifference develops. When the boother lowers his or her voice to match the visitor's, the chance of alienating the visitor is reduced. There are many clues to look for such as posture, gestures, personal space, personal greetings, speed, pace, and tone of voice, to name a few.

By matching the para-verbal and nonverbal, visitors will judge the boother in a more favorable manner. The boother and visitor now have something in common. As boothers proceed, they look for additional clues that tell them how to act.

One word of clarification: Even though para-verbal and non-verbal are adjusted to match the visitor, the boother never changes his or her level of enthusiasm for the product or service. If a prospect approaches and the person's body language says he or she is tired and irritable, the boother adjusts the para-verbal and nonverbal to closely reflect the visitor's, but on the inside the boother always remains just as passionate and enthusiastic as ever.

RAPPORT DURING INFORMATION GATHERING

The introduction was the first opportunity to learn something about the visitor. During the information-gathering process, the data bank grows considerably. The more comfortable the visitor becomes, the more information the boother will glean. Is this prospect an Edgar Dunn who can help achieve objectives or a Moe Lassis who can't? Is this visitor Emma Hope who fits the profile in all areas, but is not ready to commit, or is it Zelda Post who is looking for a job? Is this visitor Louis Fatale who asks good questions, but has no potential or Ally McMate who can become a good influence? Regardless of the role, each person must be treated with respect.

ACTION questions tell boothers who the visitors are, but it's the way these questions are answered that tell the boother how to act (see Chapter 11).

Listen

One of the most powerful tools is the skill of listening. Listening and hearing are not the same thing. Hearing is the process of deciphering noise. Listening is the process of interpreting information. The information received is twofold: the answers to direct questions (words), and the hidden data concealed in how the questions were answered (para-verbal and nonverbal).

Listen to the words:
The prospect says, "How much is that?"
The boother answers, "$3,500."
"Wow," the prospect says, "That's way too expensive."

What does the boother say next? The boother might say, "We are having a show special and offering a 20 percent discount on all orders taken at the show" or "We also have a less expensive model," or "We have an excellent financing plan where you can pay it off over the next twelve months." Which answer would have been correct? In reality, at this point in the conversation the boother does not have enough information about the visitor to know which would be the appropriate response.

The tendency is often to jump to conclusions and begin the pitch prematurely. This is a symptom of a stage 2 boother.

Clarifying is part of the active listening process, which ensures that the information received is clear and accurate. Review the ACTION questions in Chapter 11 to see how answers can be clarified. Following the ACTION questions can help build rapport.

A = Authority
You might ask, "What is your position in the company?"
"I am the owner," the visitor answers.

Who do you have here? Here's a clue, the visitor could be one of the following: Edgar Dunn, Emma Hope, or Ally McMate. You may have assumed that being the owner also means being the decision maker. This may be true in many situations; however, in others it may not. Many owners of companies pass along the decision making to managers. Asking an owner to override their manager's authority would be a mistake. Asking an owner to recommend you to a manager is more realistic. So, the clarifying question is, "Are you also involved in the selection of maintenance service companies?" Now you are clarifying.

C = Capability
Capability is a chance to create a snapshot of this visitor's situation. A good open-ended question, "Tell me a bit about your situation," should

get the visitor talking. The clarifying question is, "Who is servicing this need now?" or "What equipment are you using?" These questions will ensure the information gathering can be acted upon properly.

At this stage you may be dealing with Edgar Dunn, Emma Hope, Louis Fatale, or Ally McMate. If it is Edgar, Emma, or Ally it is important to continue to qualify, but if it's Louis who really just wants to talk about the technology, then disengage. The authority question will help immensely but you need to clarify the capability by asking, "When was your last upgrade?"

T = Time

You might ask, "When is your next 'open to buy'?" The visitor may answer, "Not until our next fiscal year which begins in April." Is this lead filed away for a May follow-up? Maybe yes, maybe no. Do they want your product in May? Is May an appropriate time to follow up? When are budgets for the next fiscal period approved? These things need to be clarified. A keen ear for detail will ensure that follow-up is timed properly. A question such as, "When is the best time for me to be in touch with you?" will usually clarify the situation.

This clarifying question will also flesh out Louis Fatale, Zelda Post, and Moe Lassis. The last thing they want is a post-show follow-up.

I = Identity

A visitor walks along and all of a sudden a stranger shouts out, "Hi Bob." The visitor looks around and doesn't see a familiar face. He is baffled. Then it happens again, "Bob, over here, you nearly walked by my booth."

A boother with excellent vision has read Bob's name on his show badge and called to get his attention. Some people like this informal friendly approach. Other people are more conservative and take offense to strangers addressing them by their first name.

Here is another scenario. During a follow-up call you say, "Hello Fred, this is Barry Siskind. I met Bob at the show and he suggested that I give you a call to talk about our maintenance services."

Fred replies, "Bob?"

"Yes," you explain, "I met Bob Smith at the trade show last Monday and he said I should call."

"Oh," Fred answers timidly, "You mean that Mr. Smith asked you to call me?"

Do you see what happened? Bob Smith runs a formal organization and calling him by his first name is not appropriate. Your presumption has put Fred in an uncomfortable position.

"But aah," you think, "this could work to my advantage. If Fred thinks that Bob and I are on a first-name basis, then I stand a better chance of getting the deal." Maybe this is true in the short term but that's not what rapport building is about. It is about building long-term relationships. Your deceit will be uncovered eventually. A better approach would be an honest one. While gathering information treat the visitor more formally at first. Then when the conversation is moving along it is appropriate to ask, "Do you prefer that I address you by your surname or would you be more comfortable on a first-name basis?"

O = Obstacles

The obstacle question uncovers reasons the visitor could or would not help your boother achieve objectives. The clarifying question helps you understand the why of the obstacle. An obstacle can derail efforts. For the less experienced boother the obstacle can sound like a conversation closer but it doesn't have to be. A bit of clarification can often reveal hidden opportunities that on first glance weren't there. Here are some clarifying questions to consider once an obstacle has been revealed.

1. *Visitor*: "We have been dealing with ABC Company, your competitor, for years."

   Boother: "Tell me what you like about their service."

2. *Visitor*: "I had a pretty bad experience dealing with your company."

   Boother: "Things change; is your decision not to deal with us absolute?"

3. *Visitor*: "I work in a remote area and I don't think you can offer
   me the level of service I need."
   Boother: "Tell me what your service requirements are."

4. *Visitor*: "We can only deal with approved vendors."
   Boother: "What is the process for getting approval?"

Get the idea? Brainstorm all the possible objections before the show
and develop clarifying questions that will help your boothers better
understand the situation they are facing. Although not all obstacles
can be overcome, sometimes simply uncovering them can be a good
learning opportunity. At other times a post-exhibit appointment is
needed so you can explore the obstacle in detail. When the obstacle
is insurmountable, thank the prospect and disengage.

N = Need

It is important to bridge from one act to the next. The need question
is the bridge. It focuses on the visitor and is a clarifying question. In
most cases this question quickly follows the approach and is the
transition into detailed information gathering. If the visitor was
asked, "What solutions are you looking for?" and he or she says, "We
are looking for ways to reduce emissions in our manufacturing
process," then you might say, "Tell me, how you are planning to
accomplish this?"

Listening to the Para-Verbal and Nonverbal

Clarifying questions give the boother more information to work with as
well as additional clues that will enhance the rapport-building process.

Everyone has a unique perspective. Some get excited about things
that others may find boring. Some are interested in details, while others want only the big picture. Some people want to get down to
business quickly, while others are happier talking first. This is an
important lesson because it reveals that visitors aren't necessarily
interested in the same thing your boother is interested in.

Rapport is about having things in common. When a conversation is one-sided and filled with details that have nothing to do with the visitor, then there is a lack of rapport. The same result happens when information is presented in a manner that is foreign to the visitor. The information may be correct, but the presentation will be inappropriate. It's like going into a fancy restaurant and ordering an expensive dish. When it arrives beautifully presented on the plate, you know it will be delicious before you put your fork to it. Imagine the same meal thrown on your plate with no regard to presentation. You might look at it and say, "What? I paid all this money for this?" Ninety-three percent of the battle is won with the presentation.

Learning to read para-verbal and nonverbal clues is not difficult. It requires keen powers of observations and a nonjudgmental attitude.

WHAT TO LOOK FOR

Messages are relayed through words, the para-verbal, and the nonverbal. While most training is focused on listening to the words, staff should spend time observing the para-verbal and nonverbal as well. This is often an unconscious process, but it is very important, and boothers will have greater control over the outcome of the interaction. There are hundreds of ways that we express ourselves para-verbally and nonverbally. Here are some examples:

- *Para-Verbal clues*: pace, tone, tempo, volume, speed
- *Nonverbal clues*: eye contact, posture, use of gestures, physical space, facial color changes

These examples are the tip of the iceberg. People express themselves through their body language. What one gesture means to one person may mean the opposite to another, so judging the meaning of the action at this point could be dangerous. While gathering information and asking the ACTION questions and the clarifying questions, the boother should read and confirm the para-verbal and nonverbal clues. This may require an additional clarifying question such as, "I sense you are uncomfortable talking about your new initiative" or "You sound really excited about this change in direction."

When your boothers are proficient at observing and clarifying, it will become second nature and that's when your staff will be working at the stage 4 level.

Empathy

Building rapport requires sensitivity—a sense awareness that includes your senses: touch, smell, taste, hearing and sight. When boothers are aware of how visitors react sensually it provides another layer upon which to build rapport. Let me explain.

Your body tells you what it needs. When you need a snack it might crave chocolate. This might manifest itself in a constant staring at the dessert table, licking your lips or dreaming of chocolate. When your body is tired it craves sleep. This might be manifested with drooping eyelids, dry mouth, lack of focus, or a queasy feeling in the pit of your stomach. When your body is giving you messages, other people also see what is going on. I recently injured my hand. I sprained a ligament between by second and third finger. It was incredibly painful and took forever to heal. The problem was that it was my right hand and every time I shook hands with someone the pain was immense. I winced and those I shook hands with were able to see it. Unless you are a professional poker player and can hide your emotions, your physiology will betray your inner thoughts.

A big part of the rapport process is becoming perceptive to other people's reactions through one of their five senses. But be careful not to mislead yourself with incorrect thoughts. Everyone is prone to interpret signals differently. When I shook hands with people they might have interpreted my wince as my discomfort at meeting people, my dislike for this person, or countless other interpretations when the only problem was my sprained finger. When you see changes in physiology, confirm them verbally. "Are you comfortable with this?" or "It looks like this one will do the job for you, Do you agree?"

As adults we learn and recognize when events trigger recognition of past events. History gives us a way to reflect, to comprehend, associate and assimilate information and data. It is what helps us put things into context for ourselves. Contextualizing is a part of rapport that is learnable. What the attendee wants to know is that what you have to offer will satisfy their perception of how they see the problem. Watch their physiology and confirm.

"What would be the most important things to you?"

"So, you want something that will...?"

Building Rapport during the Presentation

Back in the forties, psychologist Abraham Maslow developed a theory which has become one of the foundations of motivational psychology. Maslow's theory of the "hierarchy of needs" has a lot to tell us about why quality visitor care is important in today's marketplace and what we have to do to meet the needs of our visitors.

According to Maslow, human needs form a hierarchy ranging from what he called the lower order needs to the higher order needs. We do not experience a need, says Maslow, until the need below it in the hierarchy has been met, and the moment the order of need ceases to be met, attention immediately reverts to that level. This dynamic is relevant to the discussion of rapport building and taking care of your visitors. It provides an insight into understanding visitors. This is important in today's marketplace. Utilizing the hierarchy of needs is a perfect tool because it helps boothers focus their attention on the right person—the visitor.

Let's take a quick look at the Hierarchy of needs.

Our society is highly developed and its infrastructure guarantees the general survival and safety of most of its citizens. Our distant forebearers were in constant threat of freezing and starvation—we simply turn up the thermostat and open the refrigerator. We have elaborate infrastructures that ensures the delivery of food from the four corners of the world to our neighbourhood supermarket, constructs houses and apartments, supplies them with electricity and heating oil, and gets rid of waste and garbage. Most of us don't give it a second thought—all we need is the money to pay for these products and services. And in the event that we don't have the money, a vast social welfare system will see to it that we have something to eat and a roof over our head.

For our most distant ancestors, survival was an immediate, personal, day-to-day concern. In modern North America, until recently it was a rare person—the indigent poor who have fallen through the cracks of the social welfare system, survivors of plane crashes in the wilderness and so on—who were preoccupied with actual physical survival. However, political and social unrest, war, and acts of terrorism have shaken our foundation and may have reverted our attention back to this basic need.

The same is true of the second level—safety. Although, there are muggers, reckless drivers, and acts of God to fear, the rule of law and an environment which hasn't seen a wild animal on the loose for decades, makes safety one of those things we simply don't have to give a lot of attention to.

Industrial safety, product safety, environmental safety, and so on are all highly regulated. The efforts of crusaders like the Ralph Naders of the world have led to an enormous body of legislation devoted to improving the safety of everything from our babies' toys to the water we drink, the conditions in which we work, and the cars we drive. And when all else fails, we have insurance. Our situation is far removed from the state of constant danger that was life not so long ago.

Compared to early man, we've got it pretty good. Early man, spent most of his life a dead antelope away from starvation and a band of outlaws on the ridge away from losing life, limb, and everything he may come to own. For us, physical survival and safety are distant issues. By virtue of our place of birth, our lower order needs are generally satisfied. Which leaves us plenty of time to pursue the higher order needs. And that's what makes understanding so important within the visitor/boother transaction. It addresses the higher order needs. An Ethiopian who hasn't eaten for a week doesn't care if the guy who drives a truckload of emergency grain drops a bag on his head—as long as he can walk away with enough to fill his stomach. The survivor of an airplane crash who stumbles out of the bush after ten days of eating berries doesn't care if the waitress at the first greasy spoon he comes upon smiles and wishes him a nice day—as long as she brings him three cheeseburgers—quickly. For most of us, care means the "personal touch" which appeals to our need for belonging, recognition, and self-actualization. The higher up the hierarchy of needs we are placed, the more important care and rapport become.

MASLOW'S HIERARCHY AND THE RAPPORT-BUILDING PROCESS

With a little tweaking, Maslow's hierarchy can be applied to the needs of a visitor.

Survival—the Objective Need

In any transaction, the customer has a basic need—to purchase a product, gather information, or solve a problem. This is "survival" in the visitor/boother interchange—we'll call it the "objective need"— the most basic need we as servers must meet. If a visitor enters a booth and the exhibitor doesn't have what they want, that visitor's lowest order need isn't being met.

The objective need is not always a matter of buying something; it can also refer to a need for service. It could be a visitor who has ordered from this exhibitor in the past and all that's needed is the boother calling his supplier to find out why the shipment hasn't arrived and when it can be expected. It could be the woman who plans to open a better clothing store meeting a government exhibitor asking about information to register her business. In these cases, there is a purpose to the call or visit and accomplishing that purpose is the customer's objective need. If the store owner doesn't get the answer to his questions, or if the woman leaves the government office without being able to register her company, the objective needs of these customers aren't being met. Meeting the visitor's objective need is not solely the function of the boother. Quality care begins with an organization's knowing its customer and equipping itself to meet their objective needs.

At a trade show the boother can't be everything to everyone, but visitors who have a strong objective need should be helped quickly.

Here the boother's presentation will focus on one or two tactics that will help the visitor solve his or her problem.

Safety

Let's look at the visitor in a big rush to find a solution. If there is only one solution provider in town, he will be a pretty happy guy but this is rarely the case. Usually there will be a choice and even given the urgency of his need, he will want to feel safe in his purchase. He will want to know that the vendor is reputable, that they won't bungle the job and that he isn't being taken to the cleaners on price—in short, he wants to feel safe in his purchase.

Warranties, guarantees and so on will help, but the boother plays an important role in meeting this need.

Have we left the need for safety back in the Dark Ages with the cave men—not at all? Every day we grow increasingly concerned about air pollution, ground contamination, too many bad fats, too many carbs, vaccination, hastily approved pharmaceuticals, shoddy manufacturing practices, product re-calls, AIDS, SARS, runaway viruses, mad cows, sick birds, terrorists, changing climate, religious extremists, political unrest, war, cell phones and brain cancer, internet viruses, the list goes on and on. We are all concerned about something. Some of us live like monks trying to avoid the dangers of the world, while others throw up their hands and patronize their local Krispy Kreme donut outlet.

The bottom line, however, is that there are still safety needs that are best addressed by people we trust, people we like, people with whom we feel rapport. Credibility is built on trust. Boothers who don't know what they are doing, who can't or won't supply necessary information, will destroy the trust which is necessary to meet the visitor's need for safety.

When a visitor leaves your booth wondering if the promises made will be fulfilled, their safety need has not been met.

Belonging

Maslow's next level of need is belonging and this too is a characteristic need in any visitor/boother transaction. If our suit buyer is left standing waiting to be served, if the server looks down his nose at the clothes he is wearing, if his request is treated as unreasonable, the sense of connection, of being welcome is gone—and along with it, visitor satisfaction.

In the one vendor scenario, our customer will buy for lack of other choices but the next time he needs help, he will look for a vendor where he feels welcome, where he feels he fits—where he belongs.

This can be a major problem in the increasing number of exhibitors who target a specific class of buyer. The customer who enters a Rolls Royce booth and is greeted with a look that says, "The Volkswagen dealer is down the hall," is not going to feel the sense of belonging that will make the transaction an satisfying one. This need is also short circuited by the stage 2 boothers with their one-pitch-fits-all attitude.

Recognition

Recognition is the next level of need in the visitor/boother transaction. This is where we address the specific needs of each individual visitor. There are three basic types of visitor-specific needs: Those which relate to the objective of the transaction, those which relate to the transaction itself, and a general need to be treated as a unique human being with a name and history. Here is where stage 4 boothers shine. These boothers have taken the time to understand the visitor and have ensured that the presentation is targeted properly to this visitor's needs.

Objective-Related

These needs relate to the specific objective of the transaction. The needs might be a matter of the use to which the purchase will be put, the cost, the style, and the quality of the item. A visitor looking for particular products will have only so much money to spend as well as a specific use and style preference in mind. He may feel the products on display are good value for the money; he may feel that warm sense of belonging; but if he feels that he isn't being recognized as and individual, he may not place the order. Or he may buy, but go away with the feeling he was being talked down to, or simply have a vague feeling that something isn't quite right, and very likely will go looking for another exhibitor next time.

Transaction-Related

The second type of individual needs are related to the actual transaction itself and will include issues of convenience, time, and efficiency. Our visitor may want to take a lot of time to get the right product mix or may be in a big hurry to get back to the office. The visitor may love the products she sees and want to place an order right away. If the boother then insists on showing her every item in the booth when she had made it plain that she was on a tight schedule, again the visitor very likely will go looking for another exhibitor next time.

General

And finally, there is the more general need for recognition—the simple need to be treated like a human being with a name and a history. I have problems with my knees and I've been seeing the same orthopaedic surgeon for years. After a two-year hiatus, I returned to his office with a problem with my foot. "Have you been to this office before?" asked his receptionist. "Oh, yes," I answered, a little stung buy the fact that after three separate operations I wasn't remembered. "The doctor has done three operations on my knee."

"Well, the doctor doesn't do knees anymore, just feet." I breathed a sigh of relief that this time my problem was with my foot yet at the same time, I was disappointed to find that I was no longer Barry Siskind, long-term patient but a nameless foot. The importance of this level of need is illustrated by a piece of contemporary research. William Wilsted, an advisor to the accounting and consulting firm of Ernst and Young Inc, surveyed customers in the banking, high-tech and manufacturing industries. His research concluded that these customers rated "the personal touch" the most important element of service, more important than convenience, speed of delivery, or how well the product works.

Self-Actualization

Maslow's final level of need is self-actualization and in the visitor/boother transaction, self-actualization is the sum of all the other parts. If the visitor can accomplish his purpose in the transaction and go away without a glimmer of doubt or worry about it, feel that he was welcomed and that his individual needs were recognized in the transaction, then the visitor will experience a satisfaction that would not be possible if all of these levels of need had not been met.

This satisfaction is more than a matter of the visitor feeling good about the transaction. It is a matter of the visitor feeling good about himself; feeling that something in the circumstances and the chemistry of the situation brought out the best in him and that for the time it took to do this piece of business he was being himself—and the best he could be.

This isn't a feeling that most of us get very often. The boother who can bring out this feeling in us, is the boother with whom we'll be glad to do business. A boother who meets all of these needs will be one we return to happily, with courtesy and understanding. When every level of need is met in an internal situation, we work efficiently, effectively, and with pleasure, and are willing to return the service when called upon for help.

Effective rapport building, then, seeks to address every level of the visitor's needs. It is based upon the understanding that the more needs the boother can meet, the more satisfied the visitor will be, and therefore the more likely to buy and return to do business again.

If the boother fails to meet the visitor's needs, it's much easier for the visitor to walk into the competitor's place of business at a show—they are across the aisle. Visitors will leave your booth and go to the competition and compare. Alternatively, the visitor may have already visited the competition and now your staff are being compared.

Of course, not all transactions can produce magic moments of self-actualization—or can they? When we duck into the neighborhood variety store for a jug of milk and a loaf of bread, we don't expect anything but a jug of milk and a loaf of bread. Or do we? Probably not consciously. But the thirty seconds it takes to make our purchase can either be a pleasant little interlude—or not. Faced with a choice, we will inevitably return to the store where they have the special brands we like, where the milk has never been sour, where the woman behind the counter smiles and automatically reaches for our favorite brand as we walk in the door, where we can count on a joke or a brief chat if we feel so inclined. Not mystical moments, but the moments which add a little contact and quality to our lives— moments for which we will walk an extra block or pay a little more. This same principle is true on the floor where visitors attend year after year their "A" list of exhibitors with whom they have an established business relationship.

But what happens if boothers can't meet a lower level need? Does this mean that there is no point in worrying about the higher levels? The answer is "NO" and the reason is that they are looking for long-term customer relationships. Let me give you an example. I recently had some dental surgery. My first stop was the nearest pharmacy to get the painkillers the dentist prescribed before the freezing came out. The pharmacy didn't have the product the dentist prescribed and the dentist had left his office, so a substitution wasn't possible. The pharmacist couldn't answer my most basic—and very pressing—need. But he recognized the urgency of my situation and took the time to call around the neighborhood until he found a drugstore that could fill my prescription and gave me detailed instructions on how to get there. Interestingly enough, when the prescription ran out, I returned to drugstore number two to get the prescription renewed. This time drugstore number two was out of my product. The pharmacist told me to take aspirin and come back the next day. Which pharmacy do you think I'm going to do business with in the future? The first druggist couldn't meet my objective need but, because he addressed my higher order needs anyway, he won in the long run.

And that's what rapport building is ultimately about—building long-term relationships.

RAPPORT DURING THE DISENGAGEMENT

Disengaging doesn't mean an end to rapport. Some boothers may feel uncomfortable. They may think, "Gee, he really wants to talk. Won't he think me rude if I end the conversation now?"

However, during the presentation the boother had the opportunity of showing the visitor their true colors. When the visitor leaves the booth with the feeling that the boother cared, post-show work becomes so much easier.

Disengaging is like saying good-bye to an old friend. You know that you will see him or her again; it's just that this particular visit is over. Although disengaging from an old friend can tug at your emotions, you gather up the courage and do it anyway. There is a mutual respect that acknowledges that both of you have other people to see or places to go.

For some reason there is hesitancy being this direct with visitors at a show. Boothers may be concerned about seeming to rebuff them or appearing rude or disinterested. But when boothers do their job properly these excuses are the furthest from the truth. Rapport during this final stage requires the right attitude. This attitude comes from within and once firmly ingrained makes saying goodby as natural as saying hello.

Maintain Focus

Boothers are at the show for a reason. They have an objective. Your company has invested considerable resources to give them the opportunity to meet these objectives. Once they allow anyone who walks by the opportunity of moving them away from these objectives, they are harming the people who count on them the most—the visitor. Imagine attending a professional sporting event and during the middle of an important play you reach over and tap a player on the shoulder and start talking. You would quickly expect that player to say something like, "I don't have time now, I have to say focussed on the game." Success is all about staying focused on the game. When boothers maintain this focus everyone around them respects and understands what they are doing. Boothers have a job that is just as important to their organization as professional athletes, doctors, lawyers, engineers, teachers, and scientists are to theirs.

Maintain Your Professionalism

As a professional maintaining focus on the game is expected. Don't confuse rapport with friendship—it's different. Building rapport is a tool to help understand how to effectively deal with visitors. It makes long-term business possibilities possible. While being friends with the people you do business with is common, (and nice) it's important to differentiate yourself as a friend from the professional. It's important to keep these roles segregated which means a careful balancing act. There is an old saying that goes "don't do business with friends." There is some truth to this. There are countless stories about friends who have broken this rule at the cost of their friendship. This doesn't mean that it can never work; on the contrary, when the roles of professionalism and friendship are clearly defined it can add incredible joy to your work as you help friends solve difficult problems with the products and services you represent. So, how do you maintain the balance?

Be Honest

When you are talking to Moe Lassis and you really want to say, "Shut up and get outtahere!" That's not quite the level of honesty I am referring to. I am talking about being honest to yourself and your convictions.

There is a common misconception in the visitor/boother relationship which says that "The customer is always right." Sometimes they are simply wrong. They know it, you know it, and nobody is willing to speak up. It's like walking into your favorite clothing store having the salesperson tell you every hideous thing you try on looks terrific. This basic lack of honesty short circuits any chance of a long-term relationship. This assumption that the visitor is right regardless of the facts negates your needs and creates a lose-lose situation. Putting this principle into action is a difficult part of the process for most people when they assume that as long as the visitor wants to talk they have to listen.

A properly executed disengagement becomes a win-win situation because both the visitor and boother have their needs satisfied.

An act of professionalism is an assertive action, which when executed properly, is respected by those you are dealing with. Assertiveness is defined as taking care of your needs without infringing on the needs of others. By virtue of its definition, assertiveness is a valuable skill in the rapport-building process. Assertiveness is different from aggressiveness, which is getting what you want without regard to the other persons needs. Aggressive people are perceived as having a need for control. This can lead to a deterioration of any relationship. It's important to understanding the difference between controlling your environment in an exhibit situation and controlling the relationship. Aggression can be perceived as a put-down. The same holds true for aggressiveness's polar opposite—passiveness. A passive approach often means you are victimized by the other person who gets what they want with little regard to your needs. Passive people generally do not take responsibility for what is happening to them. They in fact become silent martyrs throwing up their hands and saying, "What can I do?" And they do nothing. Both aggressive and passive behaviours lead nowhere. This is not the stuff that a successful business relationship is built on.

Here are some aggressive, passive, and assertive responses that you might use when disengaging with the six potential booth visitors. You be the judge. Which response leaves the visitor with the best feeling about his or her visit and maintains the level of rapport that you have been so careful to build?

Edgar Dunn

Aggressive approach: "Okay Edgar, I now have the information I need to complete the proposal for you. I'll get back to you as soon as it is ready."

Passive approach: "Thanks Edgar. Did you want to expand more on your concerns about quality?"

Assertive approach: "Thanks Edgar for spending time at our booth. I have enough information about your situation, and I have given you some information about the specifications of our new product. Let's take this to the next step and set up a meeting sometime next week when we can get into details without the interruptions of the show."

Emma Hope

Aggressive approach: "When you are interested in going ahead with this, give me a call."

Passive approach: "If you would let me spend a few more minutes with you I am sure I can get you to see the benefits of proceeding now."

Assertive approach: "I can see this is not something you have an immediate need for. I would like to stay in touch with you from time to time to see if your situation changes."

Louis Fatale

Aggressive approach: "Let me see if I can change your mind."

Passive approach: "Well, I guess there is no point continuing our conversation."

Assertive approach: "What products are you interested in?"

Ally McMate

Aggressive approach: "When you get back to the shop, be sure to tell your boss about our new widget."

Passive approach: "I know if you just let me explain a few details you will be impressed with the quality of our new widget."

Assertive approach: "I hope I've given you enough information to feel confident about recommending that your decision makers give us a second look."

Zelda Post

Aggressive approach: "I don't have time to deal with this sort of thing now."

Passive approach: "I suppose I could try to help you."

Assertive approach: "I'm not really equipped to tell you much about employment opportunities but if you visit our website or call 1-800-job-4you, I am sure you will find the information you are looking for."

Moe Lassis

Aggressive approach: "Yes, but are you interested in buying one of our widgets?"

Passive approach: "That's very interesting, tell me more."

Assertive approach: "I have to stay focused on the visitors walking by. If I have to interrupt our conversation when someone walks in, I hope you will forgive me."

Disengaging doesn't have to mean the end of the relationship. Remember that if boothers continue the conversation long after it should have ended, they are stealing time from both themselves and their visitor.

IN CONCLUSION

Rapport buidling moves you from a stage three to a stage four boother. It is a crucial step that will ensure that you have done everything possible to achieve your objectives.

Turning Leads into Business

"Knowledge is the only meaningful resource today."
— Peter F. Drucker —

The show is over. Now it's time to see if your objectives were met and turn those leads into gold.

If your sales objective was to gather leads, write orders, or sell products, you may need to wait as many attendees make their purchasing decisions after the show. The Centre for Exhibition Industry reports that 57 percent of attendees will make a purchasing decision within twelve months, but depending on the product or service, it could be longer. If your communication objective was to reinforce your brand, create awareness, or introduce a new product, you need to be assured that the messages delivered at your booth were received and understood by the right people. Now it's time to test if your objectives were met.

SALES OBJECTIVES

I was at a trade show and met an interesting exhibitor. I was excited about his product, which had an application in my business, so I asked him to send me more information. Four months later, he called. I asked, "Why did it take you so long to get back to me?" "After the show, we were so busy processing orders that we didn't get a chance to follow up with anyone," he replied. Sound familiar?

I've heard variations of this story time and again from exhibitors who really want new business, but can't seem to find the time to follow up. The real benefit of all your hard work in planning and executing a show is lost if you do not have a solid follow-up plan.

Your first contact with a visitor should be as soon as possible after the show closes. Sometime within the first week is ideal. That's not a long time, but for visitors looking for solutions to business problems, it can seem like an eternity. They are ready for business and your products and services may be the answer. They are back in their office and excited about what they saw and learned at the show. If the timing of your follow-up coincides with their increased level of interest, the chance of receiving a positive reception is greatly enhanced. If you wait too long, you might as well have not been there in the first place.

Research confirms that show leads are superior to leads obtained with other marketing tools, for four reasons:

1. *They are serious buyers.* Ninety percent of attendees use exhibitions as their number one source of purchasing information. They come to shows for a reason. In fact, 76 percent of them have a pre-set agenda. They know what they want and who they want to see. Fifty-four percent go only to one show. That's pretty serious.

2. *They are more receptive.* Forty-eight percent need to hear from you only once to make a purchasing decision because they have already seen your products and services and know what you have to offer before your follow-up call. They have also had a chance to assess your people and, if your booth staff conveyed information properly, visitors will leave with a positive impression about your organization.

3. *They have checked out the competition.* The beauty of a show is that it is a one-stop shopping center where all the solution providers are found under one roof at one time. For a well-prepared visitor,

a show is an effective way to find new products, services, and information.

4. *They are ready to buy*. Attendees visit a show with an objective. They find and compare various solutions. Fifty-seven percent of these visitors will make a purchasing decision in the next twelve months. The onus is on you to strike while your iron is hot. In order to do your follow-up in a timely manner, your follow-up program must be in place long before the show opens. It's part of your pre-show planning. It doesn't take much to win at trade shows. A little planning and a dash of common sense and you are well on the way.

Why don't the vast majority of show leads turn into business? Research has shown that nearly 80 percent of all show leads are not handled properly. An astounding 43 percent of prospective buyers receive materials after they have made a buying decision with another vendor, while 18 percent report never receiving any materials at all. The three major reasons for this business travesty are:

- Poor-quality leads
- No follow-up resources allocated
- No one was accountable

Let's look at each.

Poor-Quality Leads
Lead quality is the number one obstacle to the implementation of a follow-up plan. Often exhibitors come home with a handful of business cards or a box filled with ballots and diligently begin their follow-up. It doesn't take long to realize that the business cards contain very little useful information. Beyond name, title, and address, what do you really know about the prospect? Each follow-up conversation now starts from the beginning. It's as if you and the prospect were complete strangers.

More often than not when you make your follow-up call, the prospect's response is, "Did we win?" Clearly, the majority of these people are more interested in the prize than the product.

No wonder salespeople get discouraged when the leads they follow up are of questionable quality. And in some cases, show leads are passed along to staff, dealers, or representatives who were not at the show. A well-orchestrated follow-up plan involves many players working in harmony, each providing the next with the information they need to do their job effectively. You need to develop an effective way of gathering prospect information that is immediate, consistent, and useful. This is where a lead card works best.

Lead cards are a formalized method of recording lead information for post-show follow-up, which you learned about in Chapter 11. Whether your purpose for exhibiting is taking orders, selling products from your booth, creating awareness of your company or product, or looking for people you can do business with after the show, lead cards are your most important tool.

Lack of Resources

A common complaint among exhibitors is that after the show they are just too busy to follow up. When you return to the shop, there are orders to fill and pressing priorities that often leave lead follow-up in a "file of good intentions." Good intentions don't get business, but applying the right resources to your follow-up program will.

The right resources don't have to be considerable. In fact, your initial follow-up can be greatly enhanced with a minimum investment of a few hundred dollars. Let me explain.

Once the show is over, your visitors return to their businesses, excited about having found new solutions to their concerns. Eighty-eight percent of these visitors have never been called on and the only way they learned about you was at the show. How long will visitors' post-show excitement last? Not long. Yes, some will contact you to place an order, but many won't because they lost your information, feel that you should be more aggressive, or they bought from the competition. A well-orchestrated first contact lets these visitors know that they haven't been forgotten.

The first step is to organize your leads into three or four follow-up categories such as immediate needs, long-term potential, no need at all, and so on. Create the categories that make sense for you. Now your job is to find an effective way of acknowledging every visitor in each category. A simple thank you for visiting, or acknowledgment that their names are being passed along to a field rep who will be in touch with them shortly, or a notification that a quotation is being developed for them can go a long way. (See the section "A Note about Privacy" at the end of this chapter on collecting information for follow-up.)

This first acknowledgment lets the visitor know the next steps. Without the acknowledgment, waiting two to three weeks seems like a lifetime. Remember that your visitor has been to shows before and may have been treated poorly in the past.

Think about your categories of customers. What you would like to say to visitors in each category? Develop your letters, e-mails, or faxes in advance of the show.

SAMPLE LETTERS

Scenario 1: An attendee has visited your booth, but there is little chance of doing business.

> Dear Visitor:
> Thanks for dropping into our booth at the XYZ show. I am glad that you had a chance to see our complete line of products and were able to learn about the various solutions we have for process engineers. I invite you to periodically visit our web site to see what we are up to and what has changed. If your situation changes and you have a need for our solutions, please call.

Scenario 2: The lead has been passed to an area representative.

> Dear Visitor:
> Thank you for visiting us at the XYZ show. I have passed along your information to your area representative, John Doe, along with the

> comments you made. He has promised to be in touch with you with-
> in seven days. If you need him before that time, please call John at
> 1-800-555-1212, or me at the number at the bottom of this letter.
>
>   We are looking forward to doing business with you in the future.
> Thanks again.

Scenario 3: A proposal is being prepared.

> Dear Visitor:
>
> Thanks for visiting us at the XYZ show. Your request is being
> processed by our quotation department. Because of the tremendous
> interest we received at the show, they have promised me that your
> information will be available within fourteen days. If you need the
> information sooner, please give me a call.
>
>   We look forward to solving your concerns in the near future.

Most acknowledgments can be handled with written correspondence
sent through mail, e-mail, or fax. You can learn your visitors' preferred contact method by asking how they would prefer to receive
information and recording this on your lead cards. The problem now
is that salespeople should be out doing what they do best—selling.
This initial follow-up, if organized properly, is a clerical job and can
be handled by temporary help who will ensure that the first response
happens in a timely manner. The expense of a few hundred dollars for
temporary clerical help will more than pay for itself in the additional
business you will receive. Once the first mailing is out, you or your
staff can follow up in a more relaxed and structured manner.

   This strategy takes care of your initial post-show contact. The
visitor knows that you are serious and has a good feeling about your
ability to follow through.

Lack of Accountability

There are two issues related to accountability: Who is accountable
for follow-up? How is it monitored?

It is one thing to give leads to a sales force or dealers and representatives. It is quite another to ensure that the leads are treated properly. They may not be taken seriously because of past experience. As we have already discussed, past experience with poor-quality leads may have de-motivated some of your representatives. Now your attention turns to the challenge of lead management.

CONTINUOUS FOLLOW-UP

The balance of your follow-up program is now closely tied to your unique selling cycle. Your sales cycle is similar to a trip map. Your trip starts from the moment you meet and proceeds through the various stops. At each stop, both you and your visitor must decide how and when the trip will proceed. If all goes well, you end up at a destination where both you and the purchaser have made a commitment to conclude the business transaction. However, getting from point A to point B is not always a straight line. On your motor trip you need to stop for gas, overnight accommodation, restaurants, washrooms, sightseeing, and so on. When you are planning a trip, you take all these diversions into account and create a map that shows you the best places to stop and the approximate time to spend at each. This also allows you to calculate your average time of arrival at your ultimate destination.

Your sales cycle follows the same logic. It is your map that will lead you to the conclusion of a successful transaction. The challenge with this map is that you have a fellow passenger who may have a map of his or her own. Your job is to coordinate both your needs and those of your customers to create a realistic schedule of events and end up at the same destination at the same time. You and your visitor will take turns in the driver's seat.

Your part of the trip should be easy to identify. Every sale is different, but there are often certain steps that are consistent from sale to sale. You know what steps you normally take to complete a transaction, which are often governed by your ability to answer some of the following questions:

- Who is the ultimate decision maker?
- What are the steps needed to get to the ultimate decision maker?
- Does your product require a plant visit to test or demonstrate the product?
- What do you know about the competition?
- Do you need a formal needs analysis?
- How do you handle specifications?
- Do you need face-to-face meetings?
- How is credit approval arranged?
- Is this a new product or replacement?
- Are there regulatory considerations?
- What objections do you need to overcome?

The next step is to uncover the customer's buying cycle. This is not always easy since your first contact may have been a decision influencer who does not have a real grasp of his or her own company's internal process. This can be further complicated when you deal with a corporation with multiple decision makers. The process begins when you qualify the prospect at the booth. Your ACTION questions (which you learned about in Chapter 11) are a great way to gather information. Now in your follow-up, you need additional information. The prospect's web site is a good starting point. You can see the corporate structure, and learn more about their business and customer base—all valuable clues you need to make your presentations relevant. With this information you can start chatting with your prospect. One of the questions many salespeople omit is, "What are the steps in your buying cycle?" Ask this early in the process and it helps you to form realistic expectations.

When you take the time to understand the customers' situation, it shows them that you care about them and that you are prepared to do things their way. Developing that level of trust in some cases is 75 percent of the sale.

The next step is to set clear objectives for each call. This means being realistic about what you ask for and expect from the client. Your road map shows you the route you must take and helps you record any detours or additional stops you hadn't anticipated.

YOUR SALES ROAD MAP

Contact	Method	Objective	Timing	Responsibility	Results
1. Post-show	Letter	Thank prospects and inform them of our next step	Seven days after show	Sales administrator	Done
2. Sales contact	Telephone	Set up meeting and gather buying cycle information	Fourteen days after show	Sales rep	Meeting set for September 23 with key decision maker
3. Meeting	Personal visit	Do a needs analysis and fill in gaps in the buying cycle	Sept. 23	Sales rep	Not able to complete the needs analysis; schedule next meeting with plant engineer
4. Meeting with engineer	Personal visit	Complete needs analysis uncover; additional steps in the buying cycle	Sept. 30	Meet with plant engineer and sales rep	Obtained all relevant information to complete the initial proposal
5. Present proposal	Personal visit	Obtain buy-in from all decision influencers	Oct. 31	Sales rep and tech support	
6. Review proposal and ask for the order	Personal visit	Obtain commitment	Nov. 15	Sales rep	

Create a road map that clearly articulates both the needs of your sales' and the customers' buying cycles.

STAY IN TOUCH

It is important to stay in touch with your trade show leads on a regular basis. Announcements, newsletters, and invitations to marketing events are useful. While these tools keep you foremost in mind among a large audience, remember to treat your personal leads with extra care. Although they will receive your mass contact information, it is often personal contacts that say a lot.

Your mailing list may include thousands of names and contacts. Your personal list is in the hundreds. Sales force automation is the process of systematizing all the information that flows between customers and sellers. Some companies have found off-the-shelf contact management programs useful. Other companies' needs are beyond the capabilities of off-the-shelf contact management programs and they look for a greater degree of sophistication and customization. Which contact management program you choose obviously depends on the size of your contact list, the number of transactions, and the budget. However, you should also consider security, reporting, performance of the database, and computational capabilities between fields. These factors and others should be examined closely before deciding what to buy. Automating your sales information should be focused on how you sell. Previously you learned about your sales cycle and the customers' buying cycles. No two companies are exactly the same. A careful examination of your needs precedes the selection of the software. Here are samples of a few considerations to be discussed before deciding on a system:

- What kind of reports do you need?
- Which activities will be tracked?
- What data should reps be able to upload and download?
- How are data shared between sales, management, sales support, production, marketing, etc.?
- How much information will be accessible?

Before you begin the process, you need to develop a similar list to define everything you want to accomplish.

Your contact management system should include information about what each contact finds interesting and appreciates. Consider sending an article from a trade magazine to a client with a note that says, "Thought you might be interested in this." Tickets to a golf show, cards for special occasions, or announcements about special activities your company is involved with are also appreciated. Often what impresses people most are those little things that show you have taken the time to stay in touch.

During a recent election I heard someone object to politicians referring to the public as taxpayers. How you treat your customers is sometimes similar. If you see them only as a source of revenue, your thinking is short term. These are real people and without them you have no business. Norman Vincent Peale once wrote, "Getting people to like you is merely the other side of liking them."

Another important factor to determine is "Whose customer is it?" Does the customer belong to the salesperson or the company? Many organizations categorize their employees into two broad categories—sales and sales support. Everyone is involved at some level in the sales process, so while the sales rep has contact with the customer, everyone else has responsibility for maintaining the relationship. If you agree that the customer belongs to the company, you must ensure that each and every contact with the customer is recorded and that each person making the contact has a level of professionalism and the skills to deal confidently with the customer.

Get your sales force on board as early as possible in the planning of your show. With a clear understanding of how your leads will provide them with much needed information and an assurance that they will be passed along to them in a timely manner, their commitment to follow up should increase.

Your contact management system enhances the face-to-face sales process, but does not replace it. It increases productivity and efficiency and allows salespeople instant access to information they need to maintain relationships with their customers.

The astute marketer will also establish systems for monitoring these leads separately from leads obtained in other marketing activities. One reason for this is to establish a true return on the show investment, which, because of long sales cycles, often isn't realized for months or years after the show has ended. By tracking the real results of your show activities, you can learn valuable information and are in a stronger position to allocate future marketing dollars.

Monitoring is often accomplished by adding additional fields into an existing contact management system. You now can create regular reports on the current status of each lead. These reports become a valuable management tool. Tracking is the only way to determine whether your show investment is really paying off.

COMMUNICATION OBJECTIVES

Recognizing and testing the communication aspect of your exhibit program is crucial for three reasons:

1. *To know what worked.*

   Think of your exhibit program as a work in process. It's not like chiseling faces on Mount Rushmore and saying, "There it is and that's that." Each time you exhibit you have an opportunity to learn what worked and what did not. By testing the effectiveness of your booth staff's communication with prospects, you uncover valuable information that allows you to continuously change your exhibit program.

2. *To know if messages are getting through.*

   Measuring a communication objective is not as straightforward as measuring a sales objective. Communications messages affect attitudes and perceptions that hopefully will lead to increased sales, but that might be over the long term. You need to know now whether the visitors you are reaching react positively toward these messages.

3. *To assess the show.*

    You have learned throughout this book that not all shows are equal. Some are better for you than others. The only method of evaluating each show is through carefully orchestrated testing.

The first step is deciding what you want to test. See Chapter 1 regarding communication objectives. Are your communication messages getting through to the right people? Testing answers this question and requires the following information:

- What was the visitors' perception before the show?
- Did the booth visit affect their perception and, if so, how?
- What was their perception after the show visit?

There are two commonly used methods of testing communication objectives.

An Exit Survey

With the cooperation of show management, an independent researcher will stop delegates at the show exit and ask them to complete a quick survey.

EXIT SURVEY
Show: _____   Date: _____   1. Do you recall visiting the ABC Company's booth at the Hardware Show? If yes, what were your impressions, if any?   ☐ Yes ☐ No   Impressions: (If they answer no, thank the delegate and move on to another.)

continued

2. Were you familiar with the extent of the ABC Company's services prior to your visit?
   ☐ Yes ☐ No

3. On a scale of 1 to 10, with 10 being the highest, how important are the following services to you?

A. ABC's twenty-four-hour support service.

Before the show	1 2 3 4 5 6 7 8 9 10	
After the show	1 2 3 4 5 6 7 8 9 10	

B. ABC's ability to provide customized solutions for you.

Before the show	1 2 3 4 5 6 7 8 9 10	
After the show	1 2 3 4 5 6 7 8 9 10	

C. ABC's in-house design capability.

Before the show	1 2 3 4 5 6 7 8 9 10	
After the show	1 2 3 4 5 6 7 8 9 10	

4. How has your perception of the ABC Company changed as a result of your visit to their booth? _____

_____

_____

_____

Telephone Surveys

Within two weeks after the event, telephone calls will be made by an independent research firm hired by your company to contact show delegates in order to complete the following questionnaire. Trying to reach all delegates is often impractical, so marketers may choose to take a random sample.

FOLLOW-UP SURVEY

Show: _____

Date: _____

1. Do you recall visiting the ABC Company's booth at the Hardware Show? If yes, what were your impressions, if any?
   ☐ Yes ☐ No

Impressions:

(If they answer no, move to question 2 and then end the survey. If they answer yes, move to question 3.)

2. Which exhibitors do you best recall? What do you recall about these exhibitors? _____

   _____

   _____

   _____

3. Were you familiar with the extent of the ABC Company's services prior to your visit?
   ☐ Yes ☐ No

4. On a scale of 1 to 10, with 10 being the highest, how important are the following services to you? _____

   _____

   _____

   _____

A. ABC's twenty-four-hour support service.

Before the show	1	2	3	4	5	6	7	8	9	10
After the show	1	2	3	4	5	6	7	8	9	10

B. ABC's ability to be better able to provide customized solutions for you.

Before the show	1	2	3	4	5	6	7	8	9	10
After the show	1	2	3	4	5	6	7	8	9	10

continued

C. ABC's in-house design capability.

Before the show   1   2   3   4   5   6   7   8   9   10

After the show   1   2   3   4   5   6   7   8   9   10

5. How has your perception of the ABC Company changed as a result of your visit to their booth? _____

_____

_____

_____

A GUIDELINE FOR CREATING YOUR FOLLOW-UP PLAN

The following is a framework for an effective follow-up strategy that should be completed and committed prior to any show. By developing a follow-up plan using these questions as a guide, you will have earned yourself a position among the meager 20 percent of exhibitors who take the time to ensure that they get value from their shows.

1. Quality of Leads

Do you have a formal method of recording visitor information?
☐ Yes ☐ No

Have you organized a pre-show briefing for your booth staff?
☐ Yes ☐ No

Is your booth designed as a lead-generating environment?
☐ Yes ☐ No

What booth activities are scheduled to help boothers attract prospects?

Literature	☐ Yes	☐ No
Promotional products	☐ Yes	☐ No
In-booth activities	☐ Yes	☐ No
Seminars	☐ Yes	☐ No
Draws	☐ Yes	☐ No
Interactive activities	☐ Yes	☐ No

Games   ☐ Yes ☐ No
Attractions   ☐ Yes ☐ No
Other   ☐ Yes ☐ No

2. Follow-up resources allocated

Do you have the right systems in place for follow-up?
☐ Yes ☐ No
Do you have the right personnel for follow-up?
☐ Yes ☐ No
Can leads be sorted in order of priority?
☐ Yes ☐ No
Are follow-up letters completed in advance?
☐ Yes ☐ No
Are there collateral materials available?
☐ Yes ☐ No

How will you keep promises made at the show?

_____

_____

What plans are in place for ongoing contacts?

_____

_____

3. Accountability

Who gets the leads?

_____

_____

How quickly are leads disseminated?

_____

_____

What do staff do with them?

_____

_____

continued

Example:
    Send literature (courier)
    Dispatch a reminder letter (mail, fax, or e-mail)
    Phone call to say information is coming
    Follow-up call to set up an appointment

How do sales staff account for their activities?

_____

_____

Who is responsible for following up with the sales reps?

_____

_____

Who is responsible for final reporting?

_____

_____

Real results aren't seen until after the show has ended. Good planning will put you miles ahead of the many exhibitors who mishandle their trade show contacts.

A NOTE ABOUT PRIVACY

The right to privacy is considered a fundamental human right. Organizations, governments, and professionals all face the consequences of people who feel increasingly encroached upon and are more guarded about their personal information. Since George Orwell introduced us to "Big Brother," people have realized that there is simply too much information that can fall into the hands of the wrong people.

Access to information was initially justified as a security measure, then quickly moved to other areas such as taxation, medical, credit, and marketing. More than forty countries and jurisdictions are working to enact laws and regulations that affect privacy. While these laws differ according to each group, the overall attempt is to deal with an ever increasing erosion of our privacy rights due to new technologies.

For our purposes the intent of privacy legislation is to limit businesses' ability to collect information and use it without permission from the individual. For the trade show exhibitor it means that personal information gathered at draws, registrations, door prizes, or at the booth must be handled in accordance with the prevailing legislation.

Companies need to be diligent in getting permission to follow up. Having said this, permission is not difficult to get. In most cases all you have to do is ask. If visitors allow you to collect personal information and know what your intentions are, you can add them to your follow-up plans. If they say no, then you can't. It's as simple as that.

When you are conducting a draw, add one more line on your ballot that asks, "Would you like one of our representatives to call you to discuss the benefits of our new product?" Or, "Would you like to receive our quarterly newsletter?"

When your staff is having a conversation with a visitor, they should ask, "Can I give you a call next week to follow up with our conversation?" or "I'd like to have one of our staff call you to ask about your impression of our booth. Would that be okay?" Many of the lead-retrieval systems used by show management include an "opt-out" box that gives visitors the option of choosing whether they can be included in follow-up activities. By asking permission, you will be working within the privacy legislation. However, because the rules change according to country, province, and state, check local regulations first to make sure you are doing the right thing. The monetary fines can be stiff, but, more important, you don't want to leave people with a negative feeling about your business practices. Everything should be aboveboard.

IN CONCLUSION
Without this crucial step of turning leads into business, you never really know if your show produces results. The benefits you receive at the event are great but the real results happen after the show is over. Whether you are looking for direct sales and leads or want to reinforce your brand or image, this section goes directly to your

bottom line. There is one more step your human resources can take; it comes from working the show from the other side of the aisle where they gather strategic intelligence

Gathering Strategic Intelligence at a Show

"It takes very little talent to see clearly
what lies under one's nose,
a good deal of it is knowing which direction
to point that organ."
— W.H. Auden —

The success or failure of any business can hinge on knowing what the competition is up to. However, a well-developed competitive intelligence program goes beyond the aspect of spying on neighbors. Competitive intelligence is all about gathering relevant information from a number of sources to guide future decision-making.

A competitive intelligence program will keep an eye on competitors, technology, legal and regulatory changes, suppliers, materials, trends, and political and economic changes.

Competitive intelligence becomes an all-inclusive program with a defined strategy, an implementable plan, and a method of gathering and evaluating information.

Trade shows are one of the best places to gather information. Opportunities are everywhere: in reception lines, walking the aisles, waiting for lunch, at seminars, hospitality events, or in the competitor's booth. There are also lots of people to talk to including industry experts, association members, exhibitors, competitors, and customers. And who are the best people to gather this information? Everyone. The trick is to develop your competitive intelligence team so that each member is chosen for his or her strengths and understands how he or she fits into your corporate big picture.

Whether your staff walk through the show during booth breaks or through a show where your company is not exhibiting, many may not make good use of the experience to gather information if they lack guidance. Trade shows are fertile ground for collecting competitive information to enhance the ongoing growth of your business. Think of your trade show as an empty field that a farmer looks at each spring. Does he see a big plot of land with nothing but acres of soil, or does he see a vista of potential crops once his seeds have been planted, nurtured, and ready to be harvested? To the untrained eye, a show is nothing but row upon row of exhibitors, but the trained professional sees unlimited potential for gathering competitive intelligence.

In *The Art of War*, the Chinese philosopher Sun Tzu says, "Hence, it is only the enlightened ruler and the wise general who will use the highest intelligence of the army for purposes of spying, and therefore they achieve great results. Spies are the most important element in war, because upon them depends the army's ability to move."

In a trade show, spying is often limited to checking out the competition. I prefer the term "strategic intelligence" rather than "competitive intelligence" because of its broader implications. To me, "strategic" implies greater depth in the search for helpful information. At a trade show, strategic intelligence involves just about everything that is going on, not just what your competitors are doing.

Competitive intelligence has its limitations. For many exhibitors, it merely indicates acquiring a competitor's brochure or "mystery shopping" at a competitor's booth. Strategic intelligence, however, is the exhibitor's opportunity to gather data on many levels, which, when packaged properly, produces a wealth of information that can become an integral part of any organization's planning process.

You may want to focus on the trends in the marketplace or what new products or services your customers are looking for. Your strategic information might include information about the quality of the show, names of the up and coming stars in your industry or general scuttlebutt about who is doing what to whom. Whatever you are interested in learning, it is imperative to communicate that need to your team.

In addition, there is also the opportunity to gather smaller bits of information such as rumors and gossip about the who's who in your industry. This is like hunting for diamonds. In fact, often major discoveries await you as the result of a conversation with some loose-lipped show attendee. So, your team needs to be constantly aware of gathering these sound bites.

YOUR STRATEGIC INTELLIGENCE TEAM

Various people in your organization—from entry-level employees to the CEO—as they walk through shows, might be interested in being part of your strategic intelligence team. Shows are full of all kinds of information, so any conscientious employees who want to advance themselves or increase their knowledge of the industry can tackle the show. Even shows that are not in your business sector have value. Your employees attend all sorts of shows from the home-and-garden variety to highly specialized technical conferences. Much can be learned from every experience. Now, imagine having this army of covert information gatherers at your disposal and envisage their collective power once they are organized into a cohesive group with common goals.

You can also recruit outside resources to join your strategic intelligence team. Good customers or suppliers, for example, might find products, ideas, and trends for you if you ask. All they need to know is what you are looking for.

YOUR STRATEGIC INTELLIGENCE PLAN

Step 1: Set Up Definitions and Objectives

Before undertaking a strategic intelligence campaign, it is important to identify the issues the program will illuminate. This goes to the core of your organization's need for information to answer questions that determine future actions. In developing your strategic intelligence plans, you need to ask two questions: Where are you going? And what do you need to get there?

Where Are You Going?

By looking at your competitor's products and services and closely scrutinizing new organizations entering your market, you can get a better idea of where the market is heading. But to compete successfully, you also need to understand your own capabilities. The old expression, "You don't know where you are going until you understand where you've been," holds true. Past performance is a great indicator, but it's more than just your perception of past performance that matters. You also need customer feedback. This information gives you important clues to the second question: What do you need to get there? Your strategic intelligence research should uncover not only what your competitors are doing but also how they are doing it. A strategic examination should include the following:

- What have your competitors given up to go in this new direction?
- How has this direction affected customer perception?
- How do the staff feel about the new direction?
- How much disruption has it caused internally?
- Is the potential worth the cost?
- Has your competitor read the market correctly?

The deeper you delve into questions like these, the more meaningful your search for information becomes. Each member of your strategic intelligence team gathers bits of data, which can be fitted together to form a complete picture.

Strategic intelligence objectives strike at the core of the organization's marketing and product development needs. The information ensures that the corporate direction is on track and helps minimize the number of surprises.

Here are some sample objectives for gathering strategic intelligence:

1. Learn effective exhibiting techniques.
2. Gather information about competitors.
3. Assess the show potential.

4. Determine audience quality.
5. Meet with show management.
6. Assess industry trends and direction.
7. Meet with other exhibitors.
8. Attend industry functions.
9. Meet with industry experts.
10. Visit the media center.
11. Find foreign buyers.
12. Increase your company's visibility.
13. Find new customers.
14. Discover new uses for existing products and services.
15. Find potential partners.

Similar to our discussion of objective setting when working at the booth, having too many objectives in gathering information can be counterproductive. Get focused by narrowing your list of objectives to four or five items that will be most beneficial. Then it is crucial to prioritize the list, starting with what's most important to you. For example, if you have trimmed your list to the following objectives, you might have ranked them in this order:

1. Assess the quality of the show.
2. Learn about competitors' exhibiting techniques.
3. Learn about new trends.
4. Meet with industry experts.
5. Find potential partners.

The next step is to quantify each objective. Your criteria may look like the following:

1. Assess the quality of the show.
      Create a list of specific questions to ask:
      • all exhibit staff during the last day of the show
      • a predetermined number of selected visitors
      • show management

2. Learn about competitors' exhibiting techniques.

    Visit certain identified exhibitors with a list of specific infor-
    mation you want to uncover or observations you want to make
    about their exhibit.

3. Learn about new trends.

    Determine which particular trends you want more details
    about, identify which exhibitors would be the best to approach,
    and develop a list of questions.

4. Meet with industry experts.

    Define what type of information would be most important
    and who might be the best source.

5. Find potential partners.

    Which delegates or exhibitors are likely to have the highest
    potential for becoming customers of your product or service?
    Decide whom you want to approach and determine the best
    places and ways to approach them.

The last step is to simplify the list by saying that items 1 and 2 represent your "A" list and the others represent your "B" list. We will come
back to this a bit later.

Step 2: Do the Research

There is no point in chasing an objective that is unattainable. During
your research, ensure that your objectives are realistic. Research
comes down to two questions: What are you looking for? And where
will you find the answers?

What Are You Looking For?

Obviously, the more information you can gather, the better, but not
just any information. Focus your efforts on gathering sufficient relevant information to ensure that you can meet your objectives. There
are many places at a show where you can do this.

1. *The exhibitors*: Review the list of exhibitors to see if your major competitors are in the show. Are there exhibitors who might be potential partners either in terms of bringing a product or service to market or simply initiating joint marketing activities at the show? This also gives you a good overview of the show and how things are laid out. For example, is the show segmented by sector or are exhibitors you're interested in widely dispersed? In a large show, this enables you to target certain areas rather than having to walk through the entire show.

   Who are the major players and how much space do your competitors hold?

   If you are not exhibiting, such information provides clues as to whether or not it might be a show worth exhibiting at in the future.

2. *Conference program*: The conference program in the show directory lists the dates, times, topics, and presenters of the various keynotes, workshops, and lectures. To learn more about what's going on at the show, the conference program is a must. Other sources of learning potential are in-booth seminars conducted by many exhibitors. These are occasionally listed in the conference agenda or on the individual exhibitor's web sites. The conference agenda will be a strong indicator of the traffic pattern you might expect as a potential exhibitor. For example, concurrent workshops might result in slow times on the show floor. They are often the best times to walk through the show.

3. *Industry activities*: Many shows are owned by or affiliated with industry associations. Shows are a source of revenue for the association and also opportunities when all the major players are gathered together under one roof. Many associations use these occasions to hold meetings, organize a director's summit, or other education-, relaxation-, or networking-related activities. If your objective falls into any one of these categories, knowing about these industry events is crucial.

4. *Show layout*: An effective show visit necessitates a familiarity with the "lay of the land." You need to know the location of exhibitors as well as the seminars, special programs, floor-staged events, rest areas, hospitality suites, and even bathrooms. This overview allows you to plan your visit effectively so you can concentrate first on those areas of most value to you. Once again, it's a matter of looking for clusters of activities.

5. *Timing*: The time of year during which the show is scheduled may be applicable to your business's needs. Buying cycles vary according to the industry. Obviously you want to be in front of your customers when they are most receptive to new ideas. When is the most advantageous time for you to approach your customers? Since the timing of events during the day is also important, a potential exhibitor must also identify the peaks and valleys of traffic booth scheduling. It's also important to ensure that your walking plan doesn't omit any important activities.

6. *Other*: Don't limit your search to these five things. There are always other bits information that will help you meet an objective. Your list may include obtaining contact information on speakers, industrial personnel, show management, and key industry individuals; visiting local sights for future hospitality information; checking out hotel and ground transportation; and registration procedures and restrictions.

The Sources

Once you have identified what you need to know and are confident that your objectives are realistic and achievable, you need to identify the sources available to help you meet your goals. You may need more than one source of information to satisfy your various strategic intelligence purposes.

Internet

Most shows have a dedicated web site through which you can learn everything from the overall show theme to which companies are exhibiting. What's covered and the level of detail vary by show. Some sites will be very helpful and easy to navigate, while others aren't. You can do a lot of pre-show work on-line, including registering for educational sessions, booking special hospitality events, and even conducting a virtual tour of the show.

Web technology and higher computer speeds enable show organizers to make their show sites more meaningful and easier to navigate. They can provide direct links to individual exhibitors, details about the conference program, on-site registration, and perhaps a copy of the floor plan. Well-maintained sites change constantly, so once you have found the home page for the show you are interested in, bookmark it so you can go back every few weeks for updates. The show directory is the single most important source of information. It is the "show in a book." Other sites include those hosted by governments or associations. They are more general in content, but can be helpful when researching industry and other data.

Trade Associations and Publications

Trade associations and trade publications are a great source of information. In many cases the association and magazine are integral parts of the show. Calendars are posted on association web sites and in their publications, but there is more to using these sources. Often representatives from the association or publication have already seen the show or are planning to attend. Talk to them about what you are doing and ask them for helpful tips. Let them be your eyes and ears. Their anecdotal information can be of tremendous value.

Public and Private-Sector Specialists

In some cases, you may be able to contact a specialist from one of the various levels of government who has some experience with the show you are targeting. There are also specialists in the private sector, such as your suppliers, who can also be good sources of advice.

Your Customers

Don't overlook your customers. They can be valuable members of your strategic intelligence team. Since customers may have access to areas of the show from which general visitors may be excluded, they can give you important information. I am not suggesting that you ask your customers to spy for you, but learning about their findings from prior shows they have attended can be very helpful. Ask them questions such as: "Which shows do you attend?" "What is your objective at each show?" "How do your peers view the show?" An open dialogue with your customers can help you achieve your objective.

Step 3: Assign Responsibilities and Create a Schedule for Your Strategic Intelligence Team

Your CEO may have access to events that your technical folks do not. On the other hand, customer service professionals may have more interest in certain workshops than manufacturing people. Everyone has strengths and weaknesses. We all have areas we find more interesting than others and subjects in which we are more knowledgeable. Sending a non-technical person to a highly technical presentation is clearly a waste of time.

The easiest method of delegating responsibility is to give people choices. Prepare a list and have individuals sign up for those events and tasks that they feel best equipped to handle.

STRATEGIC INTELLIGENCE TEAM RECRUITMENT SCHEDULE

Please sign up for the event you are most interested in participating in and the areas of responsibility you would like to tackle.

Event	Objective	Date	Team Member	Responsibility

Step 4: Gathering the Information

At this point you know what you want (your objective) and where you plan to get it (the event or person). You have also determined that your objective is realistic by doing the necessary research. The next step is to gather the information you need to achieve your objective. Start with a list of specific questions. For example, if your objective is to assess the quality of the show and you plan to ask exhibitors and attendees, your questions may include:

- How does this show compare with others you have attended?
- Were you able to meet your objectives at this show?
- Did you feel that the show's promotional activities were sufficient?
- Did you have any difficulty navigating this show? If yes, please explain.
- How helpful were show staff?
- Would you visit/exhibit at this show again?
- How helpful were the workshops/seminars/hospitality?

If your objective is to learn about your competitors' exhibiting techniques and to have your staff make a visual evaluation, you may set up a survey that will include some of the following questions:

- How much space did this exhibitor have?
- How would you rate their location?
- How many booth staffers did they engage?
- How would you rate their professional image?
- How did they treat booth visitors?
- What amenities did they include in their display?
- Did the staff handle themselves professionally?

You can create your own questions based on your objective and the people you plan to approach.

Your show notebook is a key resource for recording information. You can use a simple three-ring binder with separate sheets for each contact you are about to meet and the responses you receive. Each sheet has room for all your questions and is organized by objective.

SHOW NOTEBOOK

Name of show: _____

Date: _____

Objective: _____

Contact information: _____

Name: _____

Company: _____

Booth number: _____

Phone/mobile: _____

Appointment day/time: _____

Questions	*Responses*
1 _____	1 _____
2 _____	2 _____
3 _____	3 _____
4 _____	4 _____
5 _____	5 _____

Completed by: _____

These sheets are distributed to your strategic intelligence team according to their sign-up preference.

Step 5: Develop the Walking Plan

In step 1 you put your objectives in order of priority and grouped them into an "A" list and a "B" list. You are now ready to put this step into action. Developing a walking plan starts with a close examination of the floor plan. You can download this from the show's web site before your visit or find it in the show guide you receive when you register. The floor plan is a schematic that identifies the booths, special events, and amenities of the show. It is well worth your time to study it carefully before you head out to the show floor.

With your show notebook in hand, plot each contact on your show floor plan. If you are seeing specific exhibitors, then indicate an "A" or "B" in the booth location. If you are meeting someone at a pre-designated spot, you can indicate the meeting place. If you are hoping to see people with whom you have not set up an appointment, then see if you can identify a likely place such as a seminar room, hospitality suite, media room, or show office where you can meet with them.

As you complete your walking plan, a pattern will begin to emerge. You should now notice clusters of "A" and "B" priority items. These clusters will guide the direction of your show visit. The purpose of developing a walking plan is to make your limited time as productive as possible. There is always the risk of having your visit cut short, so each minute counts. Your clusters will also include other meeting areas such as seminar rooms or visitor lounges. Your entire walking plan is now on paper before you venture onto the show floor.

Step 6: Strategic Intelligence Overlap

The bigger the show, the tougher the challenge. Working with your strategic intelligence team is a great way of minimizing lost opportunities. As we discussed previously, each member of your strategic intelligence team has his or her own set of objectives or a portion of an objective they are sharing with other team members. Just because one objective has been assigned to one person does not relieve the rest of the team from all responsibility for that objective. Knowing what each member is looking for keeps all team members alert for opportunities that someone else might have missed. This means that team members should walk through the show, alert for opportunities beyond their assigned objectives.

You should also schedule time to meet with colleagues to compare observations. This could be at a breakfast meeting or at the end of the day when your team is ready to relax and share information. If you are exhibiting at the show, you can discreetly set up a bulletin board or message center in your booth where members can check in periodically during the day or do it by e-mail. Team members can send e-mail throughout the day through their laptops or PDAs.

Step 7: Combat Information Overload

Information overload is the scourge of all show visitors—too many seminars to attend, exhibitors to visit, and special activities in which to participate. A typical visitor is simply inundated with information from all directions. According to psychologists, the average person can cope with about five bits of information at one time. Anyone who has ever visited a show knows that the amount of information available exceeds this number by several multiples.

Eliminating information overload completely is not realistic, but it is possible to minimize its effect. The first step is in your preparation. With a well-constructed, strategic intelligence plan of action, you will be much more focused and less likely to be overwhelmed by all the available potential at the show. The second step is to ensure that your walking plan includes time-outs to recharge your batteries. When you are plotting your "A" and "B" priorities on the floor plan and creating your show notebook, add the approximate time you want to spend at each stop. Don't try to time this down to the exact minute. Once you are talking to someone, you may find that spending an extra few minutes is very productive. I suggest that you block out your time in fifteen- or thirty-minute intervals. With the time element added to your floor plan, you can include regular breaks, perhaps every two hours. This means that at the end of a two-hour interval, you do something else—attend a seminar, have coffee, get some fresh air, meet up with other members of your strategic intelligence team, and so on. The old expression "a change is as good as a rest" has never been more applicable than when you apply it to your walking plan. Listening attentively to others at a show can be very tiring.

Another tip is to become an intelligent accumulator. Often visitors have a tendency to gather lots of free goodies—brochures, premiums, etc. Once you get back to your office, you might not have the time or the interest to sort through them. The solution is simple—take only what you really need. If it is really important, take it, or you can ask the exhibitor to send it to you after the show. If the information you want is available on the exhibitor's web site, record the appropriate information and look it up later.

Step 8: Evaluate Your Results

In step 1 you articulated a clear, measurable objective. This last step gives you an opportunity to see if you have achieved it. First, gather all the completed sheets from your show notebook and analyze the responses. Next, set up a post-show debriefing where everyone on your team has an opportunity to get together to compare results. By assembling all team members, you have an opportunity to add to the information you have gleaned. Listening to another person's observations often acts as a trigger for things you saw. If getting together in person is difficult, the same result can be accomplished through e-mail or a conference call.

The agenda should include the following:

- Did you see everyone on your list?
- Did you get the information you were looking for?
- Did you encounter any obstacles?

This last question is helpful for your strategic intelligence team as they make plans for the next show.

Each team member should prepare a written report that summarizes his or her observations. With these observations in hand, decisions makers can get to work. It is really helpful when you give the team feedback on how their intelligence gathering helped the decision-making process. It is helpful for the decision makers to make recommendations for future intelligence-gathering efforts. The more information flows back and forth, the more valuable it becomes.

IN CONCLUSION

No two organizations are the same. Each has its strengths and weaknesses. A strategic intelligence strategy will take these into account and utilize the strengths of the corporation to create a plan that has maximized efficiency at a minimum of cost.

Index